QUANTUM
CONSCIOUSNESS

About the Author

Peter Smith is the creator of the quantum consciousness experience and founder of the Institute for Quantum Consciousness. For years he has researched expanded states of consciousness and their connection to quantum physics.

Peter has always been inspired by his work at the Michael Newton Institute for Life Between Lives Hypnotherapy (also known as TNI). He was president of the institute from 2009 to 2018 and trains LBL practitioners and teachers in different parts of the world. In 2013 Peter was presented with the Peggy Newton Award for outstanding service to TNI. He now serves on the board as director of the Newton Legacy. He speaks regularly at various conferences and on radio programs and has participated in a number of documentaries both in Australia and overseas.

Peter's background is as an executive in the Australian banking industry. He served for over two decades with one of Australia's leading banks before starting his own change management consultancy, focusing on values-driven organizational transformations across Australia, Asia, and the United Kingdom.

Peter undertook postgraduate studies at the Australian Graduate School of Management at the University of New South Wales and studied different forms of hypnotherapy in Australia and the United States. He has published a number of articles on quantum consciousness, hypnotherapy, and Life Between Lives therapy and is one of a group of coauthors of *Memories of the Afterlife*, the final book in the best-selling Life Between Lives quadrilogy.

Peter and his partner Melina are based in Melbourne, Australia. He runs a busy clinical practice in the eastern suburbs and spends much of his time writing. Peter and Melina also travel widely to both promote and teach for the Institute for Quantum Consciousness.

JOURNEY *THROUGH*
OTHER REALMS

QUANTUM
CONSCIOUSNESS

PETER SMITH

Llewellyn Publications
Woodbury, Minnesota

FIRST EDITION
Second Printing, 2019

Cover design by Shira Atakpu
Interior illustrations by the Llewellyn Art Department

Llewellyn Publications is a registered trademark of Llewellyn Worldwide Ltd.

Library of Congress Cataloging-in-Publication Data
Names: Smith, Peter (Peter Bernard), author.
Title: Quantum consciousness : journey through other realms / Peter Smith.
Description: First edition. | Woodbury, Minnesota : Llewellyn Publications, 2018. | Includes bibliographical references.
Identifiers: LCCN 2018014506 (print) | LCCN 2018030929 (ebook) | ISBN 9780738755656 (ebook) | ISBN 9780738754932 (alk. paper)
Subjects: LCSH: Parapsychology. | Consciousness--Miscellanea. | Metaphysics--Miscellanea.
Classification: LCC BF1031 (ebook) | LCC BF1031 .S637 2018 (print) | DDC 130--dc23
LC record available at https://lccn.loc.gov/2018014506

Llewellyn Worldwide Ltd. does not participate in, endorse, or have any authority or responsibility concerning private business transactions between our authors and the public.

All mail addressed to the author is forwarded, but the publisher cannot, unless specifically instructed by the author, give out an address or phone number.

Any internet references contained in this work are current at publication time, but the publisher cannot guarantee that a specific location will continue to be maintained. Please refer to the publisher's website for links to authors' websites and other sources.

Llewellyn Publications
A Division of Llewellyn Worldwide Ltd.
2143 Wooddale Drive
Woodbury, MN 55125.2989
www.llewellyn.com

Printed in the United States of America

Also by Peter Smith

Hypnoenergetics—The Four Dimensions:
An Overview of the New Approach to Hypnotherapy
That Is Inspiring People Around the World

For Melina...
who stands hand in hand with me
at the place where our personal universes
join, blending into my soul.

Contents

Disclaimer *xi*

Acknowledgments *xiii*

Foreword by Jane Jacobs *xv*

Preface *xix*

Introduction *1*

Chapter 1: What Quantum Physics Is Telling Us   11

Chapter 2: Ripples of Wisdom from the Consciousness
        Community   25

Chapter 3: Quantum Consciousness Emerges   53

Chapter 4: The Journey Through Your Personal Universe   73

Chapter 5: The Realm of Stored Consciousness   81

Chapter 6: The Realm of Alternate Consciousness   89

Chapter 7: The Realm of Parallel Consciousness   111

Chapter 8: The Realm of Interdimensional
        Consciousness   125

Chapter 9: The Realm of Eternal Consciousness   139

Chapter 10: The Quantum Consciousness Experience   145

Chapter 11: Changing the Landscape of Planet Earth   165

Chapter 12: The Evolved Landscape of Planet Earth   181

Conclusion: An Evolved Consciousness for Humanity   *189*

Resources   *199*

Bibliography   *201*

Disclaimer

This book is not intended to provide medical advice or to take the place of medical advice and treatment from your personal physician. Readers are advised to consult their doctors or other qualified healthcare professionals regarding the treatment of their medical problems. Neither the publisher nor the author takes any responsibility for any possible consequences from any technique or practice to any person reading or following the information in this book.

Acknowledgments

Authoring a book is a labor of love that would not be possible without the involvement of others. I have learned that the ones to keep close to you are those who carry the energy of loving support. These are the people who keep you going as you travel the writer's journey of discovery, excitement, and inevitable frustrations, which in hindsight become the greatest teachers.

My eternal thanks to Melina, for her loving encouragement. She brings color and energy to my purpose in this existence. Her patient initial editing, research, and willingness to partner with me as we became the first quantum consciousness test subjects has expanded our personal universes to a higher purpose for our planet and what lies beyond.

Our thanks to Jane Jacobs, who brings new life to our models and approaches and evolves this offering in a way that would not be possible without her. She is worthy of Remembering.

I offer gratitude to my teacher, mentor, and friend Dr. Michael Newton and his wonderful wife, Peggy. Many years ago I dreamed of meeting him and then had the great joy of working with him for over a decade before his passing in 2016. I remember life-changing conversations in airports, riding in the car, over a meal, and by phone and email. I've heard it said that in the generations that follow when people hear of the work of "Dr. Newton," they will think of Michael and not Isaac. This would simply be appropriate for such a remarkable soul.

To the early courageous explorers who came to our first workshops to try out new techniques and energies, make new friends, explore their personal universes, and help us accumulate the initial research behind this emerging modality—thank you for trusting us.

To those of you who have allowed us to tell your stories in these pages—John, Robyn, Sarah, Paul, Clare, Richi, Annette, Suzanne, Doreen, Melina, Philippa, Nadia, Liz, Melissa, and Jane—thank you so much for sharing.

And to all those other beings out there who support us and our evolution, thank you.

FOREWORD

In the 1300s there lived a poet by the name of Hafiz. Hafiz writes of much beauty in his poem "My Brilliant Image" as he reminds us that the incredible light we each hold at the core of our being is ever-present, even through our loneliest and darkest moments.

Hafiz's offering holds the Remembering of who you truly are as much as it holds the forgetfulness of who you believe yourself to be. The words carry the absence of becoming the "light of your being," the absence of earning, evolving, or attaining. There is a whispering of the Remembering of the truth of who you are now, who you always have been, who you always will be. And in the stillness between the words, there rests a gentle call to come home to yourself.

Hafiz stands among the many great teachers throughout the ages who have carried a simple core message, offered in a myriad of ways. You are enough. You are the light at the end of the tunnel. You are that which you seek. You are connected to all that is because you *are* all that is.

In the times we are in now, what is known as "the veil" is very thin, dissolving moment by moment. Every single interaction between what appear to be the opposite sides of the veil are dissolving the very belief in it. The veil's apparent construction was formed through the belief in separation. This singular belief, the belief in being apart from the universe, from all creation, from each other, and, most of all, from ourselves has been the singular cause of human suffering throughout the ages. The origin of the belief in separation hardly matters. Now, simply, the belief is beginning to be seen for what it is, revealing that it is not and never has been the truth. You are not apart from the universe; you are a part of the universe, an expression of all that is.

The paradox is that the long history of human suffering has been the catalyst to draw closer to a memory held deep and safe in the human heart. This memory has been at the core of all striving and yearning throughout the ages of humankind. The longing to be in the peace of truth again has been the driving force behind the status attained, the material gained, the mountain climbed. Yet an emptiness has prevailed. It's as though the emptiness has echoed to the memory held, with a cry of "There must be more" and "This is not it"—a "knowing" that you are not home. You cannot call for something that you have not known. No one truly forgets.

As the interactions between what appear to be the different sides of the veil increase, more light can be shed on what truly doesn't exist, revealing only what does. At the time of writing, things are moving very fast. What is it that is moving fast? Awareness and insights are being offered as never before, limiting beliefs surfacing in order to be revealed as the illusions that they are. Knowing there is a better way, rather than longing for it. A growing sense of dissatisfaction with the way things are. The dissatisfaction heralding an awareness, a Remembering of the better way.

Humanity is in the greatest time of its history, and you are an important part of it. This time in history cannot happen without your presence. You are among many and you are not alone. You are being supported and are supporting the ending of the great suffering, bringing about its ending by your own Remembering. As you so do this, you reflect to others their Remembering, being the mirror so that others can see themselves in you.

Quantum Consciousness offers you so much. It offers you a glimpse of your magnificence, of your unlimited capacity to live and explore within and beyond time, space, and other dimensions.

This book is important, as it articulates the foundations, the theory, and clients' stories of the quantum consciousness experience. To explain in simple terms and remain true to the essence of something that is so intricate requires exceptional skill and understanding. Peter offers that in this book and is supported by the generosity of the clients who willingly share their experiences with you as the reader.

The astonishing light of your being is shining away what does not exist, revealing only what is.

Rest now, in the Remembering of all this. Come home to yourself ... Be.

Jane Jacobs
Quantum Consciousness Facilitator and Coach

PREFACE

There are two worlds that we depend upon to help us understand our place in the universe: the world of science and the world of spirituality ... both with their own version of "truth."

For centuries these worlds have been separated by philosophical, logical, and even indoctrinated viewpoints, though a revolution is taking place and is starting to bring these opposing landscapes toward alignment.

Science started to change about a century ago with the discovery of quantum mechanics. Suddenly, the smallest scientific environments imaginable became even smaller, and we began to understand that at the level of subatomic particles, the laws of classical (Newtonian) physics that had served us well for hundreds of years no longer worked at all! Slowly, we discovered that we are part of the fabric of the universe and that the small toe on our left foot is made up of the same particles as a planet. We discovered that ultimately we are all connected into a divine matrix of energy, potentially made up of tiny vibrating strings that underpin reality as we know it. We discovered that there are other dimensions, alternate realities, parallel universes, and that it may have all started with a "big bang." The biggest surprise for scientists was that these theories could all be proven through mathematics, experimentation, or both.

Those two bastions of credibility, good old-fashioned (and some new) mathematical formulas and the repeatable experimentation in closely controlled environments, showed clearly that our view of the universe was wrong.

In parallel, a different group of people had been exploring consciousness in many and various ways. These consciousness pioneers were doing their own experimentation and were busy researching and validating past-life recall (sometimes under hypnosis, sometimes not), near-death experiences, astral traveling experiments, and the realm between incarnations. These expanded states were showing that consciousness does not need a body to survive and could either leave the body for a while and return or recall an out-of-body experience while still in the body. The doctrines offered through the traditional religions suddenly seemed to be helpful merely up to a point, before the thirst for personal experience took people into their own journey of discovery.

Quantum scientists tell us that we are energy, consisting of subatomic particles, and that the entire universe is our home.

Consciousness researchers tell us that we are an energy that shifts, changes, and travels unbound by time and space.

Both are right: we are quantum consciousness.

We are a window to a dynamic and unfolding universal journey. Simply put, we are a human portal waiting to be released into the fabric of the cosmos itself.

The purpose of this book is to help people *Remember*: to remember that we are part of creation, part of a greater energy, and that the remembering of this through a personal experience is all it takes to change a life.

This book will offer an amalgamation of thoughts, new ideas, and concepts, the sharing of great work from other consciousness explorers and the results of case studies undertaken in clinical practice by the quantum consciousness facilitator network.

Ultimately, we intend to bring new thought to a troubled planet. To move from a world of uncertainty to a world of possibility. To create a different future from an emerging perspective that heralds an awakening for humanity. To bring the quantum realm and expanded states of awareness together.

Welcome to quantum consciousness.

INTRODUCTION

There is an archetypical story called the *hero's journey*. Joseph Campbell identified the archetypal hero's journey in universal myth. Appearing in the narrative structure of literature, movies, and fireside tales throughout history, it can be employed and engaged with as inspiration for becoming an agent of one's own life journey, reaching one's ultimate potential, and finding fulfilment. Ultimately, there are three stages to the story: the leaving of a familiar world to answer a call, the navigation of a new, unfamiliar world of adventure, and, finally, the return to the start point as a person forever changed.

My story is not a hero's journey, as I have failed to deliver on the third step. You see, I'm never coming back. I've found my world of adventure, and I've decided to stay there.

For some years in my practice, I have offered my clients an experience called *life review*. In a loving and supportive healing environment, we establish a trance state and travel to the future, to the end of their lifetime. In this wise future state, we look back on a life that continued under the current energy and intention and the client reflects, "Did I achieve all that I came here for?" and "What are my greatest achievements and my deepest regrets?"

Ultimately, the intention of such an experience is to know your *pregrets*. In other words, to understand from that perspective what didn't go as planned. Then back here in the now, we make the changes that bring courage and inspiration to move forward in life under a new intention.

However, all this has changed since the startling discovery I have made, that time and space are not what we understand them to be. In the life review, perhaps we are glimpsing a real future outside the realms of time and space, established through an expanded state of awareness. Then we are able to create an alternate reality through a conscious life-changing shift in our linear timeline back here. At that point we simply move into the preferred reality and live the life we really wish to live.

The original understanding was founded on a world based on the Newtonian view of the universe. The new understanding is based on the view of a quantum world. Which do you prefer?

As humanity we need to make a huge decision. Do we remain in the realm of cause and effect, blind to the latest findings in quantum physics that tell us we are creators of our own realities, or do we have the courage to undertake the hero's journey, by expanding our awareness into new territory? To realize what ancient texts, shamans, and the consciousness movement have been trying to get across to us all along, that we are creators of our own destiny, that we form our own reality? We are a world of possibility and not one of certainty. We are a collection of subatomic particles that evolve to the intentions of our own consciousness based on the quantum view.

In the movie *The Matrix,* Morpheus offers Neo a choice. He can take the blue pill and remain in blissful ignorance of the simulation of reality, or he can take the red pill and find out what the world really is.

This book is for people willing to take the red pill.

Quantum Consciousness offers some of the basics of quantum physics as a springboard into expanded states of awareness so our consciousness can be free from the human intellect and other restrictions of the human condition. What you will learn from this book is that your multidimensional magnificence is closer than you think. From others' stories of personal transformation comes the insight that our greater magnificence is well within our reach.

All of us have a deeper guidance that is available if we simply stop and listen. Perhaps you could call this a soul. It is like a little GPS that guides us on our journey and lets us know when the turns are approaching. (These days, though, I sense the *G* is for *galactic* rather than *global*.)

This GPS will kick in at a certain point when we are approaching a fork in the road, often helping us decide on a direction that may seem more courageous or less so. At times, only in hindsight is the courage apparent, more often than not when someone takes the trouble to point this out to you. You pause, and then an insight comes and suggests that the life event recalled may have been one of those unrecognized courageous moments. We all have them, and life can be as full of them or as empty of them as you choose, though I encourage you to seek them out, as they are strongly linked to adventure and also to the fulfilment you accumulate on the journey of life.

A Little Bit of Background

History records my birth as a reasonably unspectacular event in 1964 in the western suburbs of Sydney, Australia. I was born to middle-class, hardworking parents and was the youngest of three children. A stable childhood, with echoes of loving kindness and strong traditional values, offered me a firm foothold in life. The seeker aspect within me quickly emerged, finding the world of books a way in which to fill the void left by a mind looking for answers and seeking a higher truth. Books about paranormal phenomena, UFOs, Bigfoot, and so on, balanced by adventure stories, offered hope and inspiration, somehow reflecting greater dimensions of life yet to be uncovered.

One of my first experiences of consciousness came with an out-of-body experience in my early teens, when I awoke floating above the house and thinking how strange it was to see the backyard from that angle. I remember reflecting on the fact that the roof gutters really needed the leaves taken out of them and that our trampoline looked very small indeed. Instantaneously, I found myself back in my body and lying in bed, spared further experiences of gutter leaves and with the trampoline back to normal size.

Around this time, the pearls of wisdom from my traditional Christian religious upbringing seemed to lose their luster. They held great intentions, to be sure, in regard to love, peace, and forgiveness, though much remained unanswered. One thing that seemed illogical to me was the fact that if we had an immortal soul that lived for all eternity, then why would it only come down here once for about eighty or so years? Surely that would be just a blink of the eye for such an immortal being. I was told by my Sunday school teachers to read the Bible and find my own answers. That really didn't help, so I read more science fiction.

I had always been sensitive to the energy of others, able to tune in to their feelings. This was to help me greatly in the later years when I became a therapist. I found I was able to clear my troubled energy field at times by writing poetry—catharsis by written expression born of deep reflection.

By thirty-five years of age, I was an up-and-coming banking executive, and the changes started. The first thing I recall is being shown a photograph of my great-grandfather at the same age. Surprisingly, we were identical. I had been open to the idea of reincarnation, though I had always needed the proof of my own experience. This event saw me seek the services of a past-life hypnotherapist, and I embarked on a journey of deeper self-discovery.

So I became one of those dual beings—the corporate executive by day and the spiritual seeker out of hours. The transformation picked up speed. I dropped out of the MBA year of studies the bank was offering to me and, having already dabbled in Reiki and some of the other healing arts, studied hypnotherapy instead. I became fascinated by the energy of us in human form and discovered that much I had been told about being in the world was either incomplete or just plain wrong.

The organization I worked for was doing some fascinating things in organizational and cultural change. I signed on as a champion to help lead this program, again needing personal experience to become more engaged in the wave of transformation. Another of those benchmark moments happened when during an energetic exercise, blindfolded on a paddock the size of a football field, I was able to alter my consciousness to find my buddy by tuning in to her energy field, walking past countless others and straight into her arms. It just wasn't possible without something else happening. My seeking picked up speed.

By the time I hit forty, I was out of corporate life. I'd stayed just long enough to glean some deeper learning from the banking world. The organization in which I had spent twenty-three years had a few hidden corners where consciousness was being explored. In the coming years, I explored Barrett's Seven Levels of Consciousness model, David Hawkins's Map of Consciousness (based on applied kinesiology), and Beck and Cowan's *Spiral Dynamics*. These are all evolutionary models of human consciousness showing the true potential of humanity and where we can evolve through collective intention.

I stepped into life as a clinical hypnotherapist and in parallel started a change management consultancy, helping people change at the personal level and helping organizations transform and clear the stagnant energy in their culture and open new areas of growth. I was trained and accredited in the Barrett model and took this into a number of different organizations. I started to build my own consciousness models for the first time, such as the Seven Levels of Soul Discovery and the Seven Levels of Human Connection.

At this time, I made an even greater discovery, a book that would change my life. My desire to become a hypnotherapist had been born out of my own remarkable journeys into past-life exploration. Then one day in a bookshop, while looking for a present for my hypnotherapy teacher, I paused to tune in to the many thousands of books in the store. I was drawn to the metaphysics section, and standing in front of that particular shelf, I closed my eyes and whispered, "Take me to the book I need today." I stepped forward and pulled a book by Michael Newton titled *Journey of Souls* off the shelf. It is hard to describe what happened next. A wave of knowing came over me, and I felt something open in my chest. I looked around to see if anyone else was having a strange reaction, though this seemed to be specifically for me.

I devoured this book as well as Michael's *Destiny of Souls* and *Life Between Lives* and found myself on a plane heading to the United States to learn more of this work. To summarize this field of work, documented so robustly and extensively by Michael Newton, I can simply say that he was the first to comprehensively explore and map the spiritual realm where we go between incarnations. He did this through the eyes of seven thousand clients over thirty-five years, and the beautiful exchange within this staggering body of work is that he took those people to meet their own soul, and they showed him the world of spirit. His research, so painstakingly accumulated, showed that we all return home to the same place, where we can understand why we chose this incarnation and what purpose and intent we have brought for the life we are currently experiencing. Following the publishing of his work, he then started to train experienced hypnotherapists to facilitate these same sessions, called Life Between Lives (LBL).

I became a student, a training instructor, a board member, and ultimately president of the Michael Newton Institute for Life Between Lives Hypnotherapy (TNI), a role in which I served for nine years before being asked to remain on the board as director of the Newton Legacy. The Newton Institute is a not-for-profit organization dedicated to continuing Michael's legacy to humanity. At the time of writing, LBL sessions are offered in forty countries by 220 highly specialized practitioners. This organization serves humanity in a remarkable way. The highly trained therapist network offers people the experience of awakening an understanding of their immortal identity. Therapists introduce the client to their very soul for a life-changing experience of remembering they are more than they could ever have known otherwise—all offered through the experience itself. Michael's original cases have now grown to over forty thousand globally.

Back home in Australia, I cofounded a hypnotherapy school and started to teach a pragmatic and effective form of hypnotherapy/psychotherapy using some new models and techniques creatively discovered in clinical practice with the help of courageous clients ready for deeper work.

Soon the energy called me further into a new model of consciousness that we called *Hypnoenergetics*, a modality that I created that brings energy, consciousness, and hypnotherapy together into a life-changing experience.[1] I embarked in a new direction, founding the Institute of Energetic Transformation. Hypnoenergetics brings together hypnotherapy, energy, and consciousness. It was a culmination of all I had done to date

---

1. More information can be found in my book *Hypnoenergetics—The Four Dimensions* or at www.hypnoenergetics5D.com.au.

with those three fields of endeavor, now wonderfully aligning into a multilayered consciousness model. My book *Hypnoenergetics—The Four Dimensions* introduced the physical presence, the emotional landscape, the spiritual being, and the energy field as the four dimensions that align with the conscious, subconscious, superconscious, and collective consciousness of our being. The experiences offered under this philosophy bring a limitless and profound approach to healing that has surpassed my previous experience of clinical hypnotherapy from both a therapist and client perspective.

Then I discovered more...

Quantum physics drifted into my line of sight, offering validation of many of the energetic experiences I was uncovering. Three years of research ensued, and I reached a place where I was no longer dealing with an advanced approach to hypnotherapy; instead, I was moving into the energy of consciousness and the universe itself.

More models emerged, embracing theories of alternate realities, parallel lives, and eternal consciousness. Flipcharts started to fill most walls in the house as the models were tested and then validated clinically. My life partner, Melina, had joined me in this work, and other therapists also became involved. We held exploratory workshops in 2013 and 2014, before sending these therapists out to road test the theories. A central repository for case studies was created and continues to grow. We founded the Institute for Quantum Consciousness to take this work further through dedicated research, trainings in different parts of the world, and the support of a growing network of accredited facilitators.

Where once we offered the deeper remembering of who we are—as a child, in another lifetime, or even as a soul—now we help people remember that they are actually part of the fabric of the cosmos. They exist in different parts of their personal universe in unison, in different bodies, dimensions, and realities.

As always, I had to have my own personal experience of this journey before I could become an advocate. Now some years later, I can share that I have spoken with myself in alternate realities, connected with parallel lives, and touched my eternal consciousness. I have felt the universe itself—personally validating for myself that I am part of all there is.

If we all truly knew this and experienced that we are all one, what would it do for our troubled planet? What would it offer those who feel lonely or disconnected? How would it shape the decisions of powerful people who have the resources to change the world? What would it do to accelerate our evolution as a species?

My journey to date has brought me to this point, where I have something to share, just an offering humbly made. What you decide to do with the information in this book is up to you. You can place it on a shelf, lend it to a friend, or explore further.

Though I wonder, how would it be for you to become the portal to your own quantum consciousness? To make life-changing discoveries ... to move past the limitations of the current mindset into something new?

Ultimately, only you can explore your personal universe, and it is waiting for you.

1
WHAT QUANTUM PHYSICS IS TELLING US

I want to state at the outset that I am not a quantum physicist by any stretch of the imagination. Having studied much of the work of people who do know what they are talking about, though, has allowed me to become a "quantum fanaticist." Finally, science is beginning to understand the true, unlimited potential of us in human form, through these small-scale experiments, theoretical physics, and even mathematical validation. I see quantum physics as the science of possibility.

My expertise lies in the realm of expanded states of awareness, and for many years in clinical practice, I've offered people experiences in which they can change their lives by releasing long-held beliefs from their subconscious energy field. Others have found out firsthand that they are spiritual beings having a human experience.

More recently, with the creation and expansion of the quantum consciousness experience, we have been blending quantum potentialities with expanded states.

The part of me that really required an experience in order to feel and know my own truth needed to be satisfied. As someone who dwells on the boundary of what is accepted and not accepted, I believe we need the firsthand experience of what we can create so that experience does in fact become our reality. The human aspect of us needs to be a willing partner in union with these expanded states.

As I share findings of the quantum consciousness experience, I will offer feedback from clients in our clinical practices. Most importantly, in order for a facilitator to offer these sessions, they are required to first have the experience deeply and authentically for themselves before offering it to others. This is our concept of the *ripple effect*, a wave of evolving consciousness offered to humanity, as we move closer to the new prevailing mindsets required for transformation.

Let's dwell for a moment on the emergence of quantum physics as a baffling and remarkable science that has really changed the world. Many people remain fixed in the world of classical physics that emerged from Isaac Newton's work hundreds of years ago. His work is an amazing summary given the time, covering cause and effect in his laws of motion and a solid understanding of the motions of the heavens.

By the time quantum physics came along about 100 years ago, the world was ripe for a change of mindset. The history of quantum physics has been documented many times, and rather than repeat it again, we simply need to build on it and take the story further.

For those wanting more of the history, I can recommend the work of physicists Brian Greene, Fred Alan Wolf, and Stephen Hawking, who have all successfully translated aspects of quantum physics into something that can be better understood by the general populace. Even the 2004 film *What the Bleep Do We Know!?* was a great step in bringing quantum physics to the big screen, with animation, interviews, and a focus on entertainment.

As a member of the consciousness community, a number of things stand out to me, which are bringing science and spirituality closer together. Quantum physics now accepts that there are other dimensions, alternate realities, and parallel universes and that we may all have doppelgängers out there somewhere. All we have to do is find a way to travel to them to connect. This is where the expanded states come in. The latest thinking regarding string theory is that everything is made up of tiny vibrating strings of energy at a microscopic level, making even the atomic world look enormous. While we are yet to be able to prove this experimentally, given the scale we would need to shrink down to, mathematics confirms the theory as long as we can accept that there are eleven dimensions. So it appears we are made of the same substance as galaxies, and therefore we can safely assume we are part of all there is.

Following that remarkable discovery comes the small and well-founded leap of faith that we are the creators of our reality. The power of intention has been well documented in recent years; however, does it go far enough? What can we really create through the pure, focused intention of our ultimate and unlimited potential? At this point, some of the old religious texts and philosophical quotes make even more sense:

The Bible: "Ask and it will be given to you; seek and you will find; knock and the door will be opened to you."[2]

Rumi: "You possess the elixir of alchemy within, use it to change your enemies into friends."[3]

Buddha: "All that we are is a result of all that we have thought: it is founded in our thoughts, it is made up of our thoughts. If a man speaks or acts with pure thought, happiness follows him, like a shadow that never leaves him."[4]

Krishnamurti: "You are the world."[5]

Ultimately, there are a number of concepts in quantum physics that have enormous synergy with expanded states of awareness. In short, these four concepts build the foundation and essence of quantum consciousness. They are the observer effect,

---

2. Matthew 7:7 (New International Version).

3. Maryam Mafi, trans, "178," in *Rumi Day by Day* (Charlottesville, VA: Hampton Roads Publishing, 2014), 92.

4. Buddha, "The Twin Verses," in *The Dhammapada,* ed. Friedrich Max Müller, vol. 10 of *The Sacred Books of the East* (London: Claredon Press, 1881), verse 2.

5. J. Krishnamurti, "You Are the World," first public talk at Brandeis University, October 18, 1968, J. Krishnamurti Online, http://www.jkrishnamurti .org/krishnamurti-teachings/view-text.php?tid=19&chid=68560.

nonlocality, entanglement, and the holographic nature of the universe.

The Observer Effect

Most people who have done any reading on quantum physics have come across the *double-slit experiment*. This has been documented consistently and comprehensively in a way anyone can understand.

In the experiment, a stream of electrons was shot at a metal plate with a single slit. As these electrons moved through the slit, they formed a pattern on a screen behind the plate. The pattern on the screen seemed quite normal and represented the expected pattern, concentrated along a central line that replicated the shape of the slit through which they had been shot. Simply stated, there was only one possible way to travel through the plate, and so the electrons used it.

As a second step, a stream of electrons was shot at a plate that had two slits. The scientists undertaking this experiment were eager to see which path the electrons would choose. The findings were baffling. The screen behind the plate showed an interference pattern, characteristic of a wave passing through the slits rather than a single stream. It was as if the stream of electrons had moved as a wave and not as single particles, or perhaps it had even moved as both.

This seemed to indicate that the electrons traveled in a wave of possibility (i.e., their yet-to-be-defined state). However, when they were directly observed, they had to take a certain position and once again behaved as single particles. In his book

Parallel Universes, quantum physicist Fred Alan Wolf articulates this as follows:

> The wave of all possibilities undergoes a sudden change the instant anything physical is observed. This is called the *collapse of the wave function.* It can be imagined to occur just like a pricked balloon suddenly collapsing. The observer is responsible for the *collapse of the wave function.* She looks at the system, and the system suddenly quantum leaps into one of the possible states. The observer stands outside and when she looks in, the system observed suddenly takes on a physical value.[6]

At a microscopic level, a seed is sown and will grow to be so huge in magnitude that it has the potential to shift our collective reality as we know it. Our world is not one of cause and effect: at the quantum level, it is about self-creation and a myriad of possibilities.

In a later chapter, this will become known as the *creator effect.*

Nonlocality

Another outcome of the double-slit experiment was the apparent observation that electrons can be in more than one place at the same time, existing in a wave of possibilities, due to the phenomenon known as *nonlocality.* It is known in quantum physics that if you try to measure the mass of a subatomic particle, you can't measure its velocity. Similarly, if you measure its

---

6. Fred Alan Wolf, *Parallel Universes: The Search for Other Worlds* (New York: Simon and Schuster 1988), 53.

velocity, you can't obtain the mass. This is a principle known as Heisenberg's uncertainty principle.

Ultimately, the act of observation collapses the wave from what is referred to as the *superposition* (all possibilities) once we "know" (or decide) where that slippery particle actually does reside. However, there is another factor in this as well. Time appears to be different in this quantum world, and this gives way to a whole raft of conversations about Einstein's theory of special relativity, which posits that time is relative to the observer. Ultimately, as we will see in the following chapters, time is an illusion. I guess Einstein realized that subatomic particles don't wear wrist watches. Over the years, as many have remarked, "The only reason for time is so that everything doesn't happen at once."

So if subatomic particles don't have to be anywhere until some form of decision is made, perhaps as the result of an observer effect, it changes our view of the concrete physical world and starts to reveal hidden realities available to us. These are the same particles that make up galaxies . . . and people.

Gregg Braden, pioneer in bridging science and spirituality, articulates this concept well: "If the particles that we're made of can be in instantaneous communication with one another, exist in two places at once, live in the past as well as the future, and even change history through choices in the present, then we can, too. The only difference between those isolated particles and us is that we're made of a lot of them held together by the power of consciousness itself."[7] As we move further into

---

7. Gregg Braden, *The Divine Matrix: Bridging Time, Space, Miracles, and Belief* (Carlsbad, CA: Hay House, 2007), 45.

chapter 3, which discusses the essence of quantum consciousness, this concept of nonlocality will become known to us as *everywhereness*.

Entanglement

Einstein is said to have called the concept of *entanglement* "spooky action at a distance." This is a theory of instantaneous connection between particles across large distances. Regardless of the distance, information doesn't need to be sent from one place to another, as the connection is already there.

We need to again turn to a quantum physicist to try to understand yet another illogical application of the quantum world. In his book *The Fabric of the Cosmos*, Brian Greene tells us,

> These results, coming from both theoretical and experimental considerations, strongly support the conclusion that the universe admits interconnections that are not local. Something that happens over here can be entwined with something that happens over there even if nothing travels from here to there—even if there isn't enough time for anything, even light, to travel between the events. This means that space cannot be thought of as it once was: intervening space, *regardless of how much there is*, does not ensure that two subjects are separate, since quantum mechanics allows an entanglement, a kind of connection to exist between them. A particle, like one of the countless number that make up you or me, can run but it can't hide. According to quantum theory and the many experiments that bear

out its predictions, the quantum connection between two particles can persist, even if they are on opposite sides of the universe. From the standpoint of their entanglement, notwithstanding the many trillions of miles of space between them, it is as if they are on top of each other.[8]

Gregg Braden states it even more succinctly in his list of twenty keys of conscious creation in *The Divine Matrix*: "Key 4: Once something is joined, *it is always connected*, whether it remains physically linked or not."[9] We see examples of this in daily life all the time: when you think about someone, and they call or send a message to you in that moment or even pass you on the street.

In my clinical practice, I've had clients tell me that they knew the moment their partner or parent passed over, even having visitations by the person in energetic form to break the news to them. These experiences bring great peace and healing as part of a grieving process, showing that the principles of entanglement move beyond the physical laws of this reality as we perceive them to be.

For some years in the Hypnoenergetics modality, we have offered to clients and taught to students an experience we call *healing advocates*. In a nutshell, we use a substitute or proxy to send healing over distance to a friend or relative unable to be present in person who has been lovingly connected to them at

---

8. Brian Greene, *The Fabric of the Cosmos: Space, Time, and the Texture of Reality* (New York: Penguin Books, 2004), 80.

9. Braden, *Divine Matrix*, 33.

some stage past or present. Historically, the strongest connections we have found have been between mother and child—an interesting phenomenon, given that during the pregnancy, those two beings once were the same collection of subatomic particles, sharing, if you like, a single energy field that has then resulted in a heightened state of entanglement. In my last book, *Hypnoenergetics—The Four Dimensions,* I recount the case of Sharon, as she sent healing to her son several thousand kilometers away. She suddenly felt the need to sit up during the session, and we later discovered that family members had arrived home and disturbed his rest. He sat up and Sharon had immediately mirrored his body movements.[10]

Earlier in this book, I mentioned an energetic exercise in which as part of a personal transformation program, I was able to tune in and find my buddy on a field the size of a football oval. The interesting part of the exercise was that we were both blindfolded and there were twenty other pairs trying to do the same thing. We walked past the others, and Tracey and I moved into each other's outstretched arms with a strange sort of knowing. Over the years, this has become a great training tool I've used for therapists.

Following this course, Tracey and I stayed in this highly connected state as her work took her across the ocean to a number of South Pacific countries. On two occasions, we were able to call each other at the exact same time. On one occasion, she sent me a telepathic message to call her, and I did so immedi-

---

10. Peter Smith, *Hypnoenergetics—The Four Dimensions: An Overview of the New Approach to Hypnotherapy That Is Inspiring People Around the World* (Victoria, Australia: Barker Deane, 2011), 62.

ately, somehow receiving that message beyond time and space as we know it. Spooky action at a distance indeed.

So these connections, so deep, profound, and permanent, can exist between people whose subatomic particles have come into contact with each other.

Imagine the potential to be able to connect with other aspects of ourselves in what we see as the past, the present, or even the future. Perhaps even other realities or other parallel existences. This becomes even more possible because our subatomic particles were not only in contact with each other—they were also the same before they moved into different realities.

When the essence of quantum consciousness is discussed in chapter 3, we will come to know this aspect as *intanglement*.

The Universe as a Hologram

There has been an enormous amount of debate about whether the universe itself is a hologram. That would make us a three-dimensional projection on a two-dimensional surface. This was originally pioneered by physicist David Bohm and quantum physicist Karl Pribram decades ago. The story of their contributions to this theory and that of many others is eloquently described by Michael Talbot in *The Holographic Universe*.[11]

While more of Talbot's ideas will be discussed in chapter 2, one of the key aspects of a hologram is that any of the smallest parts contains the whole. The smallest piece can actually be the gateway to a much larger view. Take a document on a computer for example. It is a really long document, and you have suddenly

---

11. Michael Talbot, *The Holographic Universe* (New York: HarperCollins, 1996), 31, 54–55.

decided you no longer like a particular word. Let's say it is the word *remarkable*. You call up a function and ask for it to be replaced through the whole document with the word *amazing*. In an instant, you make a global substitution, and in a flash, the universe of that document completely changes. There is no sign of *remarkable* anywhere, just a great deal of *amazing*. This has happened because the information entered into the keyboard has gone everywhere within the document in order to make the difference. Every word in the document has been given this information even though only a specific word changed. This is a simple example, though the purpose of any analogy is to make something complicated and difficult easier for the present consciousness to understand. In chapter 10, which discusses the quantum consciousness experience, we will come to know this theory as *holographic healing.*

The evidence, from various sources, that we are not even close to perceiving the true potential of humanity is really starting to build. This evidence more often than not is ignored, even though it carries a level of robustness, scientific validation, and philosophical idealism that is not hampered by current belief systems.

Carl Jung postulated the theory that we could never really be ourselves until we had released two types of conditioning. The first is our childhood/familial conditioning. The second is the societal conditioning that we all unconsciously embrace. We are the absolute product of these two environments until we decide not to be so, until something within us yearns to be free, and that in itself creates an intention. It is then up to us to find a way to make the unconscious conscious.

I've come across an effective way to do this: with direct work into the subconscious, where we can release these two types of conditioning that hold us back. This is where expanded states of awareness come into their own, where we can explore the deeper realms of ourselves, whether it be by meditation, hypnosis, or another form of therapeutic practice. Having seen this done countless times, I can offer that the best results are evident in the hands of a skilled professional. The main trap with our "conditioning" is that it is precisely that. Given that this is our unconscious conditioning into limited beliefs and mindsets, it means that more often than not we need help from beyond ourselves in order to be freed.

2
RIPPLES OF WISDOM FROM THE CONSCIOUSNESS COMMUNITY

At the forefront of the consciousness movement is a group of people who are exploring and communicating about the new paradigms we can establish in order to enable humanity to transcend the current limitations of this period in history, which we ourselves have created. The following is by no means an exhaustive list of findings, people, and bodies of work, though it is further evidence of the need for us to establish fresh paradigms that open new possibilities.

Time Is an Illusion

We are driven by time in this modern era. It rules our lives as we bounce from one event to another, all wonderfully organized in a linear timeline and recorded chronologically, as a series of recent, less recent, and distant memories. We plan for the future, recall our past with either enjoyment or regret, and basically see all we have had happen to us as our story, our personal history and more or less who we are. We see time as a constant, though in reality it has already been shown that it is not.

First, from a scientific viewpoint, Einstein's theory of relativity, launched around 1913, showed that time is not constant. In 1971, experimentation validated Einstein's theory with the measured gravitational effects on atomic clocks by sending them on aircraft in different directions around the world. In a separate experiment, the aircraft were flown at different heights from the earth's surface. The tiniest of anomalies appeared in the measured time between the different clocks in these experiments. At one stage, Einstein even remarked that the only reason we have the present is to stop the past colliding with the future. This starts to shift some of that logical thinking so prevalent in our analytical mind and characterized by the brainwave pattern of beta (13 to 30 hertz). As our brainwave patterns drop into the slower ranges that characterize the subconscious mind of alpha (light relaxation, 8 to 12 hertz), theta (deep relaxation, 4 to 8 hertz), and even delta (sleep state, 0.5 to 4 hertz), the perceived constant of time becomes even murkier.

One of the most powerful applications of hypnotherapy is what we call *age regression*. There is a saying that time heals all wounds, though any hypnotherapist trained in the facilitation and release techniques of age regression will beg to differ. We will tell you that while the language of the conscious mind is "time," the language of the subconscious mind is "energy." We regularly travel to the source of childhood trauma to desensitize, reframe, and energetically release and restore the client's

Conscious mind = Time
Subconscious mind = energy

energetic field from one that is restricted and struggling to one that is free of trauma and lighter in its vibration.

As we go deeper, we can uncover other more fascinating applications of expanded states, even beyond the lifetime we know, as age regression can be extended to the period of womb consciousness and back even further into past lifetimes. While an enormous number of studies have documented evidence of reincarnation, most therapeutic practices ignore this important potential for healing.[12]

I once had a client who had a noticeable white line appear on her otherwise flushed neck whenever she was upset or agitated. We discovered that the condition related to her past lifetime as a male stock broker in New York at the time of the 1929 stock market crash. Having lost so many people's money, he had taken his own life by hanging himself. The traces of this event transcended time as we know it into the present day, causing the physical anomaly in the current body.

As we go deeper still and journey further into the Life Between Lives state, as documented by Dr. Michael Newton, we reach a state of what he refers to as *now time*, a time when the superconscious mind is activated in a way that transcends time

---

12. One of the better-known documentaries on reincarnation comes from Australian hypnotherapist and filmmaker Peter Ramster in his 1981 film *Reincarnation*. It contains historical evidence of three women taken overseas to validate their experiences of other lifetimes. Another useful reference is the work of Dr. Helen Wambach, who set about to disprove the theory of reincarnation and instead validated it from her own reckoning. She has written several books on the subject. A third useful source on the topic, the studies of Dr. Ian Stephenson of the University of Virginia, involved eyewitness accounts without the use of hypnosis.

completely, and we can review this lifetime's progress to date as well as the immortal planning behind this current incarnation.

We know from these experiences that in the expanded states of consciousness, we move outside time and space and can send a ripple of healing through time itself. The reason this becomes possible is that we blur the fabric of time while in the expanded states of awareness. We will soon show in quantum consciousness that as we move beyond time and space, blurring the boundaries between realities, we can indeed do this. However, the possibilities for healing and the accumulation of wisdom are far greater as the effect is magnified in a quantum fashion.

If ever time were seen as an illusion, it is never more apparent than in the deeper realms of our consciousness or the expanded states of being.

Furthermore, if time is an illusion, then perhaps we have to question our concept of reality as well. If we can create and alter our concept of time, then reality is not far behind.

In "Auguries of Innocence," William Blake articulates beautifully the fluidity of time:

To see a World in a Grain of Sand
And Heaven in a Wild Flower,
Hold Infinity in the palm of your hand
And Eternity in an hour.[13]

13. William Blake, "Auguries of Innocence," in *The Complete Poetry & Prose of William Blake*, revised ed., ed. David V. Erdman (Berkeley: University of California Press, 1982), lines 1–4.

Consciousness Is Held in the Field, Not the Brain

For many years, scientific researchers have been trying to discover which part of the brain houses our consciousness. It is a wonderful question, though far too narrow to fit with what is emerging as a greater understanding that tells us that not only is consciousness not held in the brain, but it doesn't actually need a body at all.

Let's start with examples of moving beyond the brain and into the body. Louise Hay's work, documented in her reference book *Heal Your Body,* has shown us that the body is a great metaphor for emotional distress. For example, Hay talks about knee problems reflecting issues around pride and ego that can be healed with an affirmation like: "I am flexible and flowing." [14]

Chinese medicine will tell you that liver problems may well relate to repressed anger and kidney problems to fear. Finally, the ultimate in mind-body connection can be found in the little-known work of German New Medicine. Dr. Ryke Hamer, a medical doctor specializing in oncology, documented thousands of cases in which physical disease started with a change in brain chemistry catalyzed by an emotional trauma. Hamer discovered this work through his own personal experience after his son was murdered. Eighteen months after this tragic event, he developed testicular cancer and was able to track this back to his own brain scans and watch the change in brain chemistry from the trauma he had experienced. He subsequently extrapolated this work to thousands of cases, including all cancers and most diseases. He

---

14. Louise Hay, *Heal Your Body* (Carlsbad, CA: Hay House, 1988), 46.

found the underpinning generic beliefs (or judgments, as he refers to them) that anchor specific diseases in the body.

In her book *The Field*, Lynne McTaggart describes an experiment by Karl Lashley, an American psychologist and behaviorist, on a group of rats. During a laboratory experiment, the rats were taught to run a maze to find a food source. In a somewhat grisly expression of how consciousness is not held in the brain, the rats had their brains burned away bit by bit until their motor functions deteriorated to the extent where they could no longer function. It was noted however, that they had continued to know their way through the maze regardless of the deliberate deterioration of their physical brains. Somehow the knowledge of the maze was held in their "field" and not in their brain alone.[15]

British biologist Rupert Sheldrake coined the phrase "morphic fields" in an attempt to explain how this information is held.[16] He felt that species of plants and animals have a collective consciousness that they share in order to know how to behave. These theories can be expanded further from the subatomic arena to whole societies in modern life. His term "morphic resonance" is defined as the influence of like upon like across time and space, and information could reverberate across generations with some form of inherent memory. It really starts to sound a great deal like quantum entanglement is occurring at the subatomic level, between groups of particles held together in a similar shape and form.

---

15. Lynne McTaggart, *The Field* (London, UK: HarperCollins, 2001), 97–100.

16. McTaggart, *The Field*, 60.

Many of us have heard about the legend of the hundredth monkey principle, popularized by biologist and zoologist Lyall Watson. As a group consciousness, a colony of monkeys learned and passed along the behavior of washing the dirt off their potatoes in the same way, even though some were separated by water from the others, living on nearby islands.

So how far does this field extend? We understand from metaphysical approaches that psychic awareness is possible and has been validated through experimentation. We know also that some of the energetic healing modalities practice remote healing and that can be validated across time and space once the conscious connection has been made. I recommend *The Holographic Universe* by Michael Talbot as a comprehensive compilation of these subjects. If we start to think about a collective field of energy that interacts and how energetic information is shared, then, as Talbot reflects, much of the paranormal does in fact look normal.

What if we leave the body behind? Can we still make contact through this field?

A few years ago, I lost a dear friend. Bernard was the owner of the clinic in which I'd practiced for many years. The clinic was his life, to the extent that at eighty-six years of age he was still practicing as a podiatrist. He was a kind man of great humor and a natural storyteller, with tales of escaping from German concentration camps in his native Holland as a teenager as well as other adventures in different parts of the world. After a period of illness, Bernard passed away, and life at our clinic continued for the other practitioners. On several occasions, we found the front door wide open, even when we were sure we had locked it the evening before. After several incidents, I asked a renowned psychic friend of mine to tune in to the clinic. She told me that Bernard was still there, moving in and out of the building and forgetting to close the door, as he had done even before his passing. One evening I sat in the waiting room and brought him into my consciousness, explaining the situation and asking for him to be a little more careful with our security. In my mind's eye, I had an impression of an apology and assurance it wouldn't happen again. I'm sure I would have looked a little strange to an observer who may have seen me that evening in deep conversation with my unseen friend, though following that chat, we never had another issue.

The Afterlife: A Growing Body of Evidence

There have been numerous documentations of near-death experiences (NDEs). Ray Moody's book *Life After Life* documents over 100 cases of NDEs in which the people who have had this experience all report amazingly similar characteristics of a sense of loving peace, a transition toward a light, and, once back in their body, a very different view of the life to which they have returned. While Moody's work has evolved over the years, his foundationary work made a strong statement about the characteristics of NDEs consistent across all cases. In more recent times, Eben Alexander's book *Proof of Heaven* has captured the hearts and minds of readers. Alexander's incredible tale of his journey into the afterlife is not just informative but also, in part, a solid and independent validation of Dr. Michael Newton's Life Between Lives work.

As part of my consciousness work, I teach how to access the collective memory of the family culture known as the *energetic lineage*. Not only is there a past-life lineage held in our consciousness, but a maternal and paternal energetic imprint is also held in our own morphic or energetic field. We are energetic beings, created through the blended energy field of two other energies. It makes perfect sense for us to comprehend that there are emotive energies stored in those fields and passed through to us.

So what is the conclusion of this growing body of evidence that comes from all kinds of different researchers, journalists, therapists, medical doctors, and scientists?

Ultimately, the field of human consciousness is something that can be accessed beyond the body, beyond time or even space. We are talking about a quantum field of energy that stores all the potential existences of who we are, can be, and have been—all of them coexisting in a timeless way.

If we are all that, then what is the true potential of us in human form as we become a portal into our own personal universe?

We Live in a Holographic Universe

As mentioned in the last chapter, there exists a theory that if we see our universe as holographic, much more becomes understandable in terms of different types of paranormal phenomena, even quantum theory. Michael Talbot has documented this very eloquently, as mentioned before. *The Holographic Universe,* his final and best-known book, is a timeless testimony and as relevant today as when it was first published in 1991. Talbot was thirty-eight at the time of its publishing and within a year had passed away from leukemia. You could argue a great loss to the world at such a young age, or you could offer that the purpose for which he came to this lifetime was complete. Either way, his writings have depth, color, and profound insight. If we embrace the holographic concept of reality, new doors open for us.

We see validation of this holographic nature in the world all around us. The principle that the smallest part contains the whole is evident everywhere. As Rumi wrote, "The drop is You; the ocean is You." [17]

Examples of this holographic phenomenon are seen in the human body through different modalities. Iridology allows us to determine potential issues in the different organs and systems by looking into the iris of a person. If the eye is the window to the soul, then the sections of the iris are smaller windows into our physiology and anatomy.

Reflexology offers a similar example, as different regions of the soles of the feet and the palms of the hands offer insight into the health of the different parts of the body. Recently, by trial and error, I've learned how to release a headache by pressing the sore point on the sole of the foot. It is something anyone can try, with permission of course.

Beyond the physical body, our consciousness also works holographically. It is as though a ripple of distress can move out into our lives and permeate the greater presence of who we are in more of an emotional way rather than a physical one.

17. Rumi, "You, You, You," in *Love's Ripening: Rumi on the Heart's Journey*, trans. Kabir Helminski and Ahmad Rezwani (Boston: Shambhala Publications, 2008), line 12.

I once had a client who told me he was incurable due to being plagued by six separate phobias. He offered me his case and told me that having tried many different approaches to find healing, I was his last resort. "I am afraid of small spaces, crowds of people, heights, loud noises, flying in airplanes, and being in multistory car parks," explained this poor person who believed he was almost beyond help.

My response was to let him know he really just had one issue—anxiety—and it manifested in six different circumstances. Once we uncovered the original sensitizing events and released the trapped energy held in the subconscious, the phobia structure simply collapsed. This ripple effect of healing washed across all the associated subconscious anxiety programs, which had created an aspect of the client that was simply trying to keep him safe, following the energetic storing of a few smaller traumas. Over time, this type of repository of energy grows larger from more and more experiences until it becomes debilitating.

Under a holographic healing method, we can wash the healed energy along a client's timeline, transmuting the trapped energy of every event that once held anxiety. These events are changed to become merely a part of the client's history and no longer trauma, allowing the client to heal.

This approach extends to deeper work in the superconscious when we access past lifetimes. On occasion a client will encounter an issue they have been working on for many lifetimes. In the between-lives state we can undertake a psychotherapeutic technique that is outside time and space. Once the client crosses over from the end of a past lifetime, they move beyond the physical realm and into *now time*. We simply call forward all from those other lifetimes who have felt this distress and help them heal in a Gestalt-type release, by reframing and dumping the accumulated energy of all those lives. Once healed, we release them back to their own parts of the client's collective consciousness. All this is possible under a holographic healing model.

The same way a ripple of trauma moves through our lives, so too can a healing vibration.

Soon we will see the nature of the holographic model in combination with quantum consciousness principles.

Our Beliefs Create Our Reality

The concept that we create our own realities is certainly nothing new. We've all heard the concepts about how attitude is "a small thing that makes a big difference" and how our thoughts become our intentions, which in turn manifest our surrounding environments.

Quantum physics has confirmed this at an even deeper level with the observer effect, discussed in chapter 1, where we see that even in the mere act of observation, we influence what is happening around us. One of my favorite quotes is attributed to Wayne Dyer: "Not only do you become what you think about, but the world also becomes what you think about. Those who think that the world is a dark place are blind to the light that might illuminate their lives. Those who see the light of the world view the dark spots as merely potential light."

While this was being discussed energetically and philosophically through many books and publications such as *Ask and It Is Given*, one person was challenging medical science with breakthroughs of great significance: Dr. Bruce Lipton. While the work of Lipton has won critical acclaim from the consciousness movement and more progressive media, he remains largely ignored by the traditional medical establishment. Note he has been ignored, though not discredited, due to his robust approach to research and his engaging, nonthreatening style. Ultimately, if Lipton's work went mainstream, it would be the equivalent of a large truck careering off the road and driving through the living room of the mental health system, while all the people in that house sat watching repeats of certain medical indoctrinations on television, based on prevailing mindsets.

Lipton's *Biology of Belief* is that truck, and the passengers in that vehicle include high-quality medical research, the principles of quantum physics, open mindsets, and a great sense of humor. I've used this book as a core text often over the years. Ultimately, in the laboratory, Lipton showed that stem cells take a certain form depending on which environment they are placed in. In short, they reacted to their surroundings beyond DNA or any of the perceived coding functions that medical science would have us believe. His stem cells took the form of bone cells, liver cells, blood cells, and so on when placed in the environment conducive to that evolution. Lipton's work releases the bonds of genetic inheritance at the cellular level, to nothing more than a relatively small propensity toward a biological outcome.

As a man of integrity and ultimately a world-renowned spokesperson for the consciousness movement, Lipton did the only thing he could do. He gave up teaching medical students, knowing that from the discoveries he had made, the curriculum was no longer valid. He now travels the world speaking to

...d letting them know that as people, we are simply
...ed Petri dishes," as I heard him remark in a presen-
...on in Sydney around 2011, reflecting the laboratory discoveries he made and extrapolating the concept to the trillions
of cells that make up our own individual colonies of cellular
consciousness.

Over many years in clinical practice, I've helped clients un-
pack deep-seated disempowering belief systems. Belief systems
that create, re-create, and hold us in a vibration of lack, isolat-
ing us from our fullest potential due to the subconscious conditioning offered to us in our formative years.

The energy of conditioning is profound, and we often miss
the opportunity to release that which holds us back. It can be
done, though, with a series of simple but critical steps.

First, you need to find it—that is, know it is actually there.
The trick with conditioning is that it is invisible to the conscious mind—we usually need someone with outside advice or
insight to spot it, and that starts with the power of intention to
go looking for it, created usually by a lack of tolerance for the
observed behavior we see in ourselves!

Second, we must understand that the belief is held subconsciously and not consciously. Cognitive behavioral approaches,
targeting the conscious mind, will more often than not have
limited impact.

Third, we need to understand that the release of that belief
is just the start. We have to understand the feeling associated
with the belief and the event or events that started it all off.
This concept of the *triangle* (event, feeling, belief) is documented
in my book *Hypnoenergetics—The Four Dimensions*. In a nut-

shell, most therapies miss the energetic dynamic, bound by this self-supporting structure of the three points of the triangle. The event, the feeling, and the belief are bound together as an energy packet, which in turn drives our unconscious behavior, and we have millions of these packets! The act of healing is to find those triangles that cluster together in themes in the subconscious and hold us back in our lives. Once identified, they can be released by a series of therapeutic and energetic interventions.

If we return to the client with six phobias for a moment, his six phobias came down to one feeling: anxiety manifesting in six different circumstances. Although, they were also anchored to one belief —"I'm not safe"—driven intensively from the subconscious at the times these phobias emerged.

There it is—very simple. If we believe with the deeper subconscious mind that we aren't safe, then we will create anxiety as a way to establish hypervigilance or stay on high alert, ready to respond to our perceived (though debilitating) need for greater safety.

So how do these belief systems start?

Remember the impact of the formative years, that first decade or so of life. As small people, we spend much of our time in lower brain wave patterns, alpha and theta, even in and out of delta as we move from sleep to awake and back again, as part of an emerging daily routine in infancy. We draw on what we are given by parents, grandparents, caregivers, and role models, and this conditioning and indoctrination into family and societal culture is impressionable, binding, and foundational.

Over the years, I've seen debilitating beliefs held in place:

- "You'll never amount to anything" ... for the client who can't seem to succeed in life and undertakes unconscious self-sabotage.
- "You can't sing" ... for the entertainer who has performance anxiety and low confidence, as well as unique and significant talent.
- "You are just like your father" ... for the client who continues the path of self-destruction of the generation before, following in the footsteps of his paternal role model.

Some of the most powerful cases of conditioning I've seen come from a medical diagnosis when a person is given a prescribed period of time before their life ends. I've heard a number of stories over the years in which the client complied with the time period given, unconsciously manifesting the beliefs of a well-meaning member of the medical profession.

We already know it doesn't need to be that way.

Every clinical trial undertaken for a new drug consists of research that includes a specific group of participants given a placebo without their knowing. We have a range of results clearly documented that show that some of these people who take the placebo experience the perceived benefits of the drug and even experience some of the side effects that were disclosed to them as part of the clinical briefing. Given we have seen this in action, just imagine for a moment the power of the mind as it draws on a belief system.

We need to ask why the placebo effect isn't being explored with the same tenacity as new drugs entering the market. Those scientific results actually show we don't need more drugs; we need a deep and profound understanding that we can heal our own bodies and that as we release the trapped energy we need to release, we heal.

Like the Lipton truck being driven into the living room of the mental health system, this would be the equivalent of the large and expensive house of the pharmaceutical industry catching fire and being burned to the ground.

Under the prevailing mindsets of our medical industries in the Western world, placebo research will never take place. To put it bluntly, there's no profit in these people healing with work on their own belief systems. Ultimately, the industry would lose all its customers, and that's just not good for business.

So, let's change the prevailing mindsets in all this to a quantum perspective and include expanded states of awareness. Let's show people that they have unlimited potential, that they don't need a body to exist. Let's tell them that all they will ever need can be found in the multiple dimensions and realities that make up their personal universe.

The way to move beyond restrictive beliefs is to transcend them. Every time Bruce Lipton steps in front of an audience, he sends that message. It is people like him, Gregg Braden, and the late Wayne Dyer who are leaders in a consciousness movement that can take humanity to the next level of our potential. All we have to do is listen to them and form our own supporting beliefs, remember that we are quantum beings of unlimited potential … and join them on the journey.

We Are All Connected as Part of a Divine Matrix

As I mentioned in the introduction, there are two worlds that we depend upon to help us understand our place in the universe: the world of science and the world of spirituality, both with their own version of "truth."

Quantum scientists tell us that we are energy, consisting of subatomic particles, and that the entire universe is our home. Consciousness researchers tell us that we are an energy that shifts, changes, and travels unbound by time and space. Both talk about a field of energy that connects all of us to the universe itself.

Gregg Braden refers to this network of energy as the "Divine Matrix" in his book of the same name. Drawing on the work of Max Planck, one of the founders of quantum theory in the 1940s, Braden articulates a case for this web of energy we are all connected to, a network that includes all there is.

He also discusses the way in which we can connect to this network, and this in turn forms a wonderful relationship between science and our own sense of spiritual and energetic self: "It's our inner language that changes the atoms, electrons and photons of the outer world. ... It's the language of emotion that speaks to the quantum forces of the universe." [18]

This reflects accurately how we are driven by our deeper triangles and how we view the world through them. A change on the inside makes a change in the world around us. So as we connect consciously and subconsciously to this network of energy, what becomes of our potential to explore it more deeply?

---

18. Braden, *Divine Matrix*, 84–85.

Braden further sites examples of the CIA's remote viewing program in the 1970s, SCANATE. He talks about extended remote viewing, accessed through altered states of awareness, to move across time and space to other geographical coordinates and report back what is found there. During the First Gulf War in 1991, success was achieved in finding missile sites without the need for a search at ground level.[19]

So, if we can interact at this level with the amazing network of energy in this Divine Matrix, then what becomes possible?

Braden's summary about the remote viewing concept articulates this potential:

> The reason why I mention these projects and techniques here is because they successfully demonstrate two things that are key in our understanding of the Divine Matrix. First, they are yet another indication that the Matrix exists. For a part of us to travel to distant locations and see the details of things that are very real without ever leaving the chair we're sitting in, there must be something for our awareness to travel through. My main point here is that a viewer has access to the destination, regardless of where it is. Second, the very nature of the energy that makes remote viewing possible shows the holographic connectedness that appears to be part of our identity. In the presence of evidence of the Divine Matrix, the old ideas of who we are and how we function in space-time begin to break down.[20]

19. Braden, *Divine Matrix,* 129–130.

20. Braden, *Divine Matrix,* 130.

So it would appear that our consciousness is free to roam where it needs to or even where it is drawn to, under a stated intention in which we engage our own observer effect.

In the quantum possibilities of time, space, and this matrix we belong to, with all the possibilities of other realms of reality that can be opened to us during expanded states of awareness, we discover that we are quantum consciousness.

We can travel as far and wide through our personal universe as our intention manifests for us, with results that may astound us.

We Exist Simultaneously in Other Realms

Where do we really exist?

There is an aspect of me in the here and now writing on my computer. I'm sitting in a chair in my place of residence not far from a lake in the city of Melbourne. My physical reality records that it is a chilly morning at 6:30 a.m., and I have just witnessed a beautiful sunrise. Beside me is a coffee cup, and I've just finished my traditional morning brew.

However, according to quantum physics, I am in other places also. I may just be dwelling in other realities too. According to Life Between Lives hypnotherapy, an aspect of my soul essence is still in another dimension, the spiritual realm.

Then what about time?

If the linear timeline, this amazing chronology of our perceived existence, is an illusion, then what about my past lives? They are no longer past but perhaps parallel. So chances are I'm there also in this now time.

Let me offer a personal experience of my own that supports being in more than one place at once.

Many years ago, as I had been fascinated by past-life work, I studied to become a hypnotherapist. As a client, I had an experience that put my hard-headed banking brain into a spin. I was taken to a vague memory of standing on top of the conning tower of a submarine during World War II. As the story unfolded, I remembered this submarine being rammed by an enemy ship after having been caught on the surface. What surprised me most was the emotion flowing through me in unison with the vision. I was troubled as I tried to integrate the experience, given the memory was vague but the feelings so real. Early one morning as I lay in bed, my deep subconscious allowed a little information to slip through, and I was given the identity of the submarine. An internet search the next day showed not just validation of the submarine's ramming but also a photo taken by a journalist on board the ship that had rammed the submarine. I sat wide-eyed, staring at that photo for a long time, as it showed the angle of ramming was exactly the same as my vision.

This event, historically recorded from another lifetime, was still sitting in my emotions. How could this be, unless there is some aspect of ourselves that transcends not only time and space but also the physical bodies that hold our present consciousness?

I became a hypnotherapist, and as many of us know, one of the most powerful aspects of our art is age regression. I found that people could move easily into the wounded childhood years to release debilitating sources of anxiety, depression, and various other disorders. At times, people would speak to me as a five-year-old would speak. Their facial expressions and features would change, and we would have access to the exact moment the trauma was recorded in the timeless archive of the subconscious mind.

Over time, I pursued my goal to facilitate past-life work for others, comfortable in the knowing that it was real from my own personal validation. Again, I found some people moving into a character of long ago, revivifying events sometimes thousands of years old with the emotions that went along with them.

As my experience grew, I started to experiment first of all with patterns. As a client left their body at the point of death in the past life, we would invoke the immortal wisdom available beyond human form, and I would ask, "Is this a pattern that goes beyond this lifetime we have been shown?" More often than not, the client would offer that there were a number of lifetimes. I started a traditional way of cutting cords to the trauma of other lifetimes across time and space, and then later I discovered you could call all the lives together, summoning them from across all of time and space to join us and undertake a healing process. We would heal them and send them back to their other lives to change their current circumstances, in some way creating an alternate life from the one that held the original issue or, at the very least, help them handle the issue better in the current timeline. Part of this therapeutic reframing was to have the client feel that they now had this number of lives supporting them rather than holding them back. We were using one of the basic principles of releasing energy of a low vibration and replacing it with that of a higher vibration. The change in these clients was both significant and sustainable.

These events have been insightful in the shaping of the quantum consciousness work, as we dabbled with all sorts of models of past lives becoming parallel lives. Once time drops away, we are potentially creating an alternate reality within these parallel lives that then carries the healed state!

That's quite a statement, and more on these concepts will be covered when we move on to those sections of this book. At the end of the day, the true benefit of these experiences is the positive change in our client. As we undertake the sacred work that ultimately serves them and allows them to heal, their personal universe and their contribution to all there is, is then offered.

One of the most remarkable pieces of work in expanded states of consciousness is, as mentioned several times before, Michael Newton's Life Between Lives work. This access to the deeper brainwave patterns in the theta range, which in turn allows access to the "superconscious," offers yet another angle on this question of existing simultaneously in other places.

Michael Newton discovered that an aspect of our soul energy stays in the spiritual realm when we incarnate. Depending on the complexity of the purpose to be undertaken during a lifetime/incarnation, a certain portion of the overall soul energy is allocated. This way the duality of the spiritual being and the human being is always maintained.

In his spiritual principles in *Life Between Lives,* Michael Newton writes, "At the moment of physical death the soul returns to the spirit world and the source of its creation. Since a portion of the soul's energy has never left the spirit world during incarnations, the returning soul rejoins with the essence of itself. Thus, spiritual learning never ceases for the soul."[21] In my own LBL practice, I have witnessed this phenomenon many times as clients share their concern that they failed to bring enough energy back to undertake the challenges of the incarnation at hand. Alternatively, they sometimes state that the largish quota of energy with which they have returned is necessary due to the intentions set for this life. Some have described the spiritual world as the place of theoretical learning and the physical realm the place of consolidating the learning into practical terms. If you like, an incarnation is like a field trip during which we really test the theories we learn in our spiritual home.

To further consolidate this concept of being in more than one place simultaneously, there is the rare occasion when a soul will incarnate into two bodies in the same linear time. Michael Newton's first book, *Journey of Souls*, gives the example of a client who is undertaking an incarnation in the USA and another in Canada in unison. These two incarnations are very separate and independent with different learnings and purposes, though they share the same soul energy. It's a little like the person who works two jobs so they can get ahead in life more quickly.[22]

While these cases remain very rare in an LBL practice, I have had two of my own. I once asked a client, who was in the deep trance state that characterizes this work, how much en-

---

21. Michael Newton, *Life Between Lives: Hypnotherapy for Spiritual Regression* (St. Paul, MN: Llewellyn, 2004), 212.

22. Michael Newton, *Journey of Souls: Case Studies of Life Between Lives* (St. Paul, MN: Llewellyn, 1994), 148–155.

ergy she had brought into her incarnation. She replied, "About 40 percent."

As I validated the number, I offered, "So 60 percent remains in the spiritual realm?"

When the client corrected me and stated, "No, 20 percent," I had to ask the obvious question about where the rest was. She responded immediately, as if surprised by the question: "In China."

This client was split between two earthly bodies in the same linear time and also still had a portion of her soul energy back in the spiritual realm. This other incarnation, male, was working in an office in China, and I was told they were destined never to meet. In fact, my client remarked, "What would be the point of that? We took separate paths so we could learn more ..."

Michael Newton has this to say about this interesting phenomenon:

> Souls in almost any stage of development are capable of living multiple physical lives, but I don't really see much of this in my cases.
>
> Many people feel the idea of souls having the capacity to divide in the spiritual world and then attaching to two or more human bodies is against all their preconceptions of a singular, individualized spirit. I confess that I too felt uncomfortable the first time a client told me about parallel lives. I can understand why some people find the concept of soul duality perplexing, especially when faced with the further proposition that one soul may even be capable of living in different dimensions

during the same relative time. What we must appreciate is, if our souls are all part of one great oversoul energy force which divides, or extends itself to create our souls, then why shouldn't the offspring of this intelligent soul energy have the same capacity to detach and then re-combine?[23]

Summary

If we amalgamate the work of all these people and even others across the field of consciousness studies, we start to form some very interesting themes in which expanded states of awareness and quantum principles come together into a consistent view of the universe.

In a nutshell, this brings science and spirituality not just to the same table—they are in the kitchen cooking the meal together. Time is malleable and changeable and can in fact become almost irrelevant once we enter expanded states of awareness. We also know that our unique consciousness is held in some form of morphic field that extends beyond the physical body into a network of energy some call the Divine Matrix.

We know that we create our own reality, even down to the cellular level, and we have discovered that we are not our genes. We are the result of our thoughts and our beliefs, and these are created from how we perceive our environments—which, by the way, we ourselves have created.

Finally, we know that we can exist in multiple places all at once, that our unique and eternal consciousness is simultaneously at the center of our present existence as well as all the

---

23. Newton, *Journey of Souls,* 155.

other places where our consciousness resides. The universe consists of the same matter at every level; the large and the small are the same. We have our own personal universe that connects us to the fabric of the cosmos itself.

We are quantum consciousness...

3
QUANTUM CONSCIOUSNESS EMERGES

Already we have seen that there is an incredible innate potential in our human form, ready to be tapped. We all experience extraordinary things from time to time, though more often than not, we surrender the importance of the experience, due to the prevailing mindsets that keep our views of reality limited.

I often have clients who feel held back by the issues in their present life or by trauma from their past. So often I've been told, "I just want to feel normal." When I ask them what they believe "normal" to be, at first I'm usually met with a blank stare. Then they try to describe a frame of mind that fits with the societal beliefs of how they are "meant to be." Something that fits a cultural system in which they don't ask questions about the bigger meaning of life; they just go about doing things in their lives that are regular, safe, and obedient in the eyes of others.

At times, we will talk about a deeper awakening they may be experiencing, perhaps what is referred to as a *dark night of the soul*, a form of existential or midlife crisis designed to shock them into an awakened state so that they can move into the purpose they came here for. The real challenge this offers to those who have the courage to wake up is that there is no going back. Once you become a seeker, by the very nature of the energy and intention of that condition, you will never be a finder. You will continue to seek and move forward on some form of hero's journey that never ends.

While this sounds scary at first, a restless life characterized by discomfort and yearning, it is in fact just the opposite. You bounce from one amazing experience to another, finding your limitations and releasing them, breaking through your conditioning and having experiences that you would never have believed possible. Once you decide to be consciously awake, you move closer to your full potential. This isn't about potential in your human form. This is about the consciousness that you already are, the expanded state of being disguised in human form: a quantum being so full of potential, connected to the universe itself.

All matter is made up of energy, and that energy has an inbuilt evolutionary program at the core of the subatomic particles that are the framework that holds a greater consciousness. On a grand scale, the universe is expanding. Galaxies are forming and reforming, stars and planets moving through a life cycle before dispersing their energy into other forms.

On a smaller scale, a seed grows into a plant and then into a tree. A baby grows to blossom into adulthood. The animal and plant kingdoms reproduce themselves all the time. Our bodies have healing systems that make us well when we allow them to, even without intervention. Everything grows and breaks down into components and then reforms. All of this is the cycle of life, the universe, and everything.

All consciousness has the intention to evolve. When we return to physical form, time after time, we are ever evolving and seeking that greater path of evolution. The philosophy of quantum consciousness is for us to know, without a shadow of a doubt, that we are part of this cycle. We are consciousness that is far beyond the limitations of human form. We are each a quantum being that lives all the possibilities of who we really are. When we become consciously quantum, we release the limitations of an existence based on the well-meaning principles of Newtonian physics.

From this understanding, the Institute for Quantum Consciousness formed the five principles of quantum consciousness:

1. *We are a human portal to all realms of consciousness.* This first principle allows us to understand that in this human form, we are merely a window to these greater states of being. Our consciousness exists in other realms in unison with this one, and rather than be marooned from those other states while in this human form we know of, we have the ability to step through that window.

2. *Our unique consciousness has the pure intention to evolve.* This second principle recognizes the innate encoded intention in our being to evolve, whether it be within this lifetime, where we go between our lives, in another incarnation, or

in an alternate reality. We are a part of the fabric of the cosmos itself, which we know continues to expand and grow in the great cycle of existence. Simply put, we hold that same intention as we are part of it.

3. *Our intention to evolve embraces multidimensional interactions with others.* Once we release our connection to human form, we can travel to these other places beyond our present consciousness. Quantum theorists confirm the potential existence of other dimensions and alternate realities. Reincarnation researchers have validated historical evidence of past lives. As we move beyond time and space, these become our parallel lives. The Life Between Lives work of Michael Newton has offered and validated experiences of the eternal consciousness.

4. *As we unite intentions with others, we amplify consciousness.* As we undertake these journeys, we can do so in the synergistic company of others, this amazing quantum entanglement amplifying our experience. We have seen from the Maharishi Effect (in which large-scale meditations for peace can lower the crime rate in a major city) that connected consciousness has a more powerful outcome. Beyond this, as we explore our personal universe and meet our other selves, they form an ever-increasing wave of united intention that sends a wave of healing and or wisdom through all realms of our personal universe.

5. *We send an instantaneous wave of evolving consciousness, rippling through our holographic universe into the fabric of the cosmos.* Finally, this is the magnificent contribution that goes beyond ourselves. This is our selfless contribution to the evolving fabric of the cosmos. As we under-

take our own evolution, we contribute to the all there is, as we are a part of it. Imagine the feeling when we create the intention to make a contribution to something far greater than we understand from our present consciousness. This is a sacred act of service to the universe itself.

These five principles encapsulate the intention and the potential of the quantum consciousness experience.

If you were drawn to read this book, then you may already know about the perceived difficulty we have releasing the limitations of our conditioning in human form. The leveraging of quantum physics, a science without limitations, is so important as a means of fertilizing the present consciousness before we undertake this journey. Though let's not get too hung up on the science—even the amazing quantum discoveries are perceived as having a need to be tested, absorbed, and proven mathematically, experimentally, or both.

In the words of astronomer and physics researcher Richard Conn Henry, "Bright physicists were again led to believe the unbelievable—this time, that the Universe is mental. According to Sir James Jeans: 'the stream of knowledge is heading towards a non-mechanical reality; the Universe begins to look more like a great thought than like a great machine. Mind no longer appears to be an accidental intruder into the realm of matter ... we ought rather to hail it as the creator and governor of the realm of matter.'" He continues, "The Universe is immaterial—mental and spiritual." [24]

So as we go one step further ...

---

24. Richard Conn Henry, "The Mental Universe," *Nature* 436 (July 2005): 29, doi:10.1038/436029a.

What if we could use just enough science to allow the present consciousness to feel comfortable with the journey through our personal universe?

Considering art versus science, by scientifically approaching art, we may lose the true potential of it, forged through creativity that goes beyond being able to be replicated. We merely need enough science to be able to accept the possibilities of our art, as every client session is a spiritual masterpiece.

I first made this statement in our initial quantum consciousness workshops to encapsulate the energy we need to embrace in order to undertake the experience. As we will see in subsequent chapters, it is the education and expansion of the present consciousness that allows this to become such a powerful journey. This becomes imperative, as we have been trained to undertake a cycle in which we experience this process:

Experience → Analyze → Accept or Reject → Integrate

Much of this draws on our alignment of the experience with two things. The first is whether the acceptance of the experience and the subsequent broadening of our view keep us safe or threaten life as we know it. The second is whether we are willing to change our view of the world in order to grow. When we are faced with the evidence, we need to make a decision. Do we stretch the boundaries of our current reality, or do we reject the experience and stay in the blindness of the prevailing mindsets?

We once thought that the earth was flat and that if we sailed past the edge, we would fall into oblivion. Then one courageous act changed the mindsets of the day: a new experience was offered, and the earliest explorers started to circumnavigate the globe. There was no choice but for everyone to accept the new truth.

When quantum physics emerged as the new science, it took existing scientists, with their prevailing mindsets, decades to start to accept that our view of the world was wrong. Having said that, we are still yet to fully change our view. If you were to sit in a high school physics class today, you would find that they still teach Newton's laws of motion. In chemistry, we study the periodic table that assumes the base building blocks of our world are atoms. It is as if the subatomic world is yet to permeate the education systems. As a result, we are anchoring the prevailing mindsets for the next generation.

When we move into the quantum mindsets in our workshops, we make a request that all participants release the limitations of the analytical cycle of experience, analyze, accept or reject, and integrate. In fact, we have just the first and second step, repeated over and over:

Experience → Accept → Experience → Accept…

How quickly would humanity evolve if we readily accepted every new experience and accepted it into our growing wisdom without any restrictive beliefs or mindsets? A world without conditioning—it's a fascinating concept.

Some may ask, what if someone loses their grip on reality? Perhaps the question to ask at that stage is whose reality do they mean? Are they saying that having an existential experience that doesn't fit with a traditional view means that someone has lost their grip on their cognitive function?

A near-death experience, a past-life regression, a Life Between Lives experience, or even someone seeing the energetic form of and communicating with a deceased loved one are simply energetic experiences outside the traditional view. Thousands of these experiences happen around the world every day. Little by little, we are being forced to accept that there is more to life than we know, and when we accept these experiences, a new depth and an enrichment of our existence in human form follows.

We still have a long way to go.

I once worked with a young girl, just seven years of age, who had been prescribed antipsychotic medication in an attempt to bring her hallucinations under control. She could see dead people at the foot of her bed every night. She benefitted from learning some strategies to understand her psychic gift rather than solely relying on medication to keep it at bay.

The Remembering

In order for us to help a client expand their state of present consciousness to the point where we can access their personal universe, we activate a *Remembering* of the quantum potential of who they really are. They need to be reminded at their core that they are full of possibilities and that they must release the prevailing mindsets that hamper the journey.

One of the ways we fertilize the present consciousness is through the Remembering:

Feeling the greater guidance that gently surrounds us now, you begin to Remember ...

Know that our journey ... starting in the here and now, ripples gently outward into the realms of your personal universe ... healing ... exploring ... serving humanity and beyond ... as your offering to all there is ...

Just relax now ... allowing any tensions to just melt away ... feeling the shift in your awareness that echoes a deeper truth at the core of your being ... We activate and empower a quantum realm that allows the embracing of all possibilities ... as you expand gently ... into your quantum consciousness.

And now allow yourself to Remember ...

In this moment, you simply know that you are a part of the greater universe, intimately connected to all there is.

With every breath, this Remembering becomes stronger as you expand ... and recall this feeling of floating outside time and space ...

With every beat of your heart, you open more and more to all that you are, have been, and will be ... all connected now as time and space are left behind ... You are simply energy, an expanding state of awareness ... part of all there is.

You feel deep comfort and peace ... from the energy that surrounds us ...

Every breath ... becomes a sacred experience ... drawing universal energy further into your being ... connecting even more strongly to all that we ourselves have

created ... Rest now ... in the Remembering all this ... Let
go and just be ...

We have found that the offering of these words has an effect
on the client that usually opens the pathways to the expanded
realms of consciousness model, the journey through their personal universe, and ultimately the quantum consciousness experience. The words encapsulate not only the possibilities we hold
in human form but also the joint intention of the client and the
quantum consciousness facilitator. As you read and feel into the
words above, you may feel that connection, that Remembering
of the greater truth of who you truly are, knowing from a deeper
place within that you are a portal to all realms of consciousness.

The Essence of Quantum Consciousness

There are four aspects that have come to be known as the *essence
of quantum consciousness*. These are based on some of the quantum principles mentioned earlier, though they are also the catalyst for deep and profound healing, amazing explorations, and
the further shifting of the present consciousness into a quantum
activation of all the possibilities in a client's personal universe.

The Creator Effect

"We are the creators of our own reality." How many times
have we heard this idea? How many times have we heard about
self-fulfilling prophecies? Even goal setting at the business or
personal level usually involves some form of visualization or
intention.

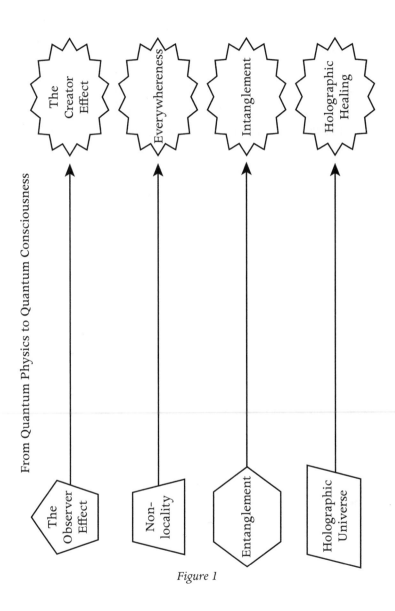

Figure 1

In hypnotherapy, we use *future pacing*. We take a client into a perceived future where all is well and they have abandoned their limiting beliefs or healed dysfunctional behavior. In his book *The 7 Habits of Highly Effective People*, Stephen Covey refers to this concept as beginning "with the end in mind." [25]

All of these approaches draw on the *creator effect*, which is offered as a deeper and more energetic evolution of the quantum principle the observer effect.

Not only are we masters of our own destiny, we are creators of our own reality. We have found the creator effect to resonate highly with the concept of free will. We choose a path either consciously or unconsciously. Again, I return to the example of the person who has anxiety, with that underlying need to feel safe. They will continue to create anxiety until they believe, without hesitation in their subconscious, that they are safe. They then create a life without anxiety simply because they are then able to.

Free will exists in abundance in human form and even beyond. As a Life Between Lives therapist, I have heard countless times over the years about the selection of a particular lifetime with all the cultural and physiological implications in order for a soul to learn new lessons. I've been told about the decision to return to this planet in the current incarnation and decisions to take on tough contracts in order to help soul friends learn, grow, and evolve their eternal consciousness. This free will extends to decisions made to take many forms in this and other

---

25. Stephen Covey, *The 7 Habits of Highly Effective People* (New York: Simon & Schuster, 1989).

dimensions through our known and unknown universe. The journey we take through our personal universe, as a subset of all there is, is rich and diverse, and I will be sharing case studies in the second half of this book.

In quantum terms, this becomes even more comprehensive as we start to talk about the creation of alternate realities, when a decision is made that creates a new path even within this incarnation. These connections remain strong because these realities have formed from the same originating subatomic particles, splitting off to form that alternate path. This concept will be discussed in detail and in case studies offered in chapter 6.

As we undertake the quantum consciousness experience, we set the following intention with our creator effect: "We are here for the creation of deep and profound healing, embracing the energy of selfless service."

"We" reflects the entangled journey of the client and the facilitator. The "profound healing" sets the intention for an experience that is life-changing. "The energy of selfless service" is layered deliberately. The facilitator holds this intention for their client. The client offers the facilitator the opportunity to undertake their purpose in this lifetime. The two of them are healing the fabric of the cosmos as the client's personal universe sends a ripple of healing into the all.

Intanglement

At first glance this looks like a typo, but it isn't. Intanglement extends the quantum principle of entanglement. We already know that we are entangled with everything around us as part of the web of energy that permeates all of creation. We also know we are part of the collective consciousness of humanity. These concepts, while incredibly inspiring, are externally focused.

Intanglement is about the internal connection to all our other selves that exist in the different realms of our personal universe. Every age we have ever been or will be is stored in our energy field. Our alternate realities are within reach and our parallel lives available for exploration. Our eternal consciousness dwells within as our loving supporter in the perfect symbiotic relationship of oneness—the spiritual being having the human experience. As we focus inward, we can access all this and more in the healing and exploring journey that is offered to us as part of our quantum consciousness experience.

Quantum physicists have experimented at length with entangled particles, as stated in chapter 2. These previously unrelated particles can make instantaneous contact across great distances once entangled. Let us stop and consider for a moment that the different aspects of our single consciousness, which are most likely made up of some form of particles (discovered or yet to be discovered), must be in even closer contact, thereby even more readily accessible to each other—more closely entangled. We have found this to be so during our research case studies, that once we acknowledge this deeper *intangled* connection, it offers ready contact and subsequent interactions with our other selves.

As we undertake the quantum consciousness experience, we set the following intention with intanglement: "We open a portal to deeper realms of consciousness."

"We" refers to the fact that we are opening this portal to the client's intangled selves while facilitator and client are energetically entangled together. "Deeper realms" embraces the expanded states that are building as we continue the journey through the client's personal universe.

Everywhereness

As the quantum principles of entanglement and nonlocality support each other, so do the quantum consciousness aspects of intanglement and everywhereness.

As we connect with our intangled other selves, our awareness is everywhere in our personal universe. We can be in many places at once, and in the same way quantum particles adopt the superposition of all possibilities, we exist everywhere our consciousness is. When we call forward a particular stored, alternate, parallel, or interdimensional intangled self using our creator effect, it is as though we collapse the wave of possibilities as one of those other selves comes forward. *Everywhereness* builds on the quantum principle of nonlocality and furthers the thought that we exist simultaneously across the realms of consciousness model. Einstein's "spooky action at a distance" just got spookier, as we have found our clients to be in instantaneous communication with these other selves. This interconnected oneness in our personal universe makes for powerful healing potential. We have the opportunity to share in the wisdom that all these others have accumulated in their realms of consciousness, as well as share healing techniques across these realms.

As we undertake the quantum consciousness experience, we set the following intention under everywhereness: "We flow with the energy to where the greatest wisdom may be offered."

As we create this intention, we are asking our greater consciousness to show us where the disruptions are in our personal universe. We seek the greatest wisdom and the greatest opportunities for healing. We call forward these other selves, creating interactions that will contribute to the raising of our vibration and the ripple effect onward.

Holographic Healing

As we embrace the holographic nature of the universe and the energy it is made up of, we have unlimited opportunities for healing.

Hypnotherapists know the power of a new belief manifesting in the subconscious. If we get to the source of an issue and release it, the cascading effect across a myriad of other programs running in the subconscious is extremely powerful. As we move through the realms of our personal universe, we send a ripple of wisdom, healing, or both through all others. This interconnectedness can, by the very nature of who we are, start a snowball effect across all our other selves.

Imagine a healing wave of unlimited potential expanding out through our stored consciousness to every age we have been and ever will be. Imagine wisdom moving from one of our wise alternate selves in another reality to all the others, and then cascading back through their own stored and present consciousness. Then we move to parallel lives, sending healing that washes back through their alternate, stored, and present consciousness.

As we undertake the quantum consciousness experience, we set the following intention under holographic healing: "As we heal in each realm of consciousness, we send a wave of wisdom through all others."

This intention takes healing to a level never before attempted. Once we acknowledge our other selves, embrace them, and offer them the healing or wisdom they most need, this intention can take effect. The most inspiring aspect of this is that the ripple we create can go as far as we wish.

When we expand to the realm of our eternal consciousness, we take our healing and wisdom with us, sending it out into the fabric of the universe as our own contribution to the evolution of all there is.

Expanded States of Awareness

Expanded consciousness, in parallel with the intention that we set, allows the client to remember what it is like to have an out-of-body experience while still in the body. The body is no longer seen as a restriction: once we know it is simply a unique expression of quantum energy particles, it becomes a portal to the other realms of consciousness.

In a final summary, the requirements for the quantum consciousness experience (QCE) include:

1. A change in the present consciousness (ΔPC) bringing a different perspective and understanding through the

modeling concepts and also the offering of the Remembering as a way to activate those quantum potentials in the client.

2. The use of the four aspects evident in the essence (E4) of quantum consciousness (QC).

- *Creator Effect:* "We are here for the creation of deep and profound healing, embracing the energy of selfless service."

- *Intanglement:* "We open a portal to deeper realms of consciousness."

- *Everywhereness:* "We flow with the energy to where the greatest wisdom may be offered."

- *Holographic Healing:* "As we heal in each realm of consciousness, we send a wave of wisdom through all others."

3. Establishment of expanded states of awareness (ESA) to move beyond the body and restrictions of the prevailing mindsets of the human condition.

So as a final comment for this chapter, we can display all of this as a visual formula, mainly just for fun, though in a way that looks just a little quantum:

$$\Delta PC + QC(E4) + ESA = QCE$$

Having now built the philosophy and conceptual framework behind the intention of the quantum consciousness experience, it is time for us to take a walk through the model itself. We look first at why someone would undertake this journey, before sharing the individual realms of consciousness we travel through and offering inspiring stories of those clients who have undertaken this journey.

4
THE JOURNEY THROUGH YOUR PERSONAL UNIVERSE

Let me begin by describing why this work is so important. Ultimately, it is inspiring to understand the holographic view of someone exploring their personal universe. The embracing of this energy ripples far beyond the individual; in fact, the portal we open during this experience brings a vibration to our world that transcends the heaviness in which we live daily. This is particularly true in the Western world, a society that is permeated by materialism, competition, and fear.

There is a separateness that is encapsulated in most of the prevailing mindsets of our communities large and small. These subconscious patterns of thought need to change. Before we can move to external cohesion in our communities, we must first remember who we are inside, so we know exactly who it is that we are integrating into the collective oneness of humanity and the universe itself.

In the previous chapter, I shared with you the four aspects of quantum consciousness that make up this offering: the creator effect, everywhereness, intanglement, and holographic healing.

I offer to you that the true potential of this work is the rediscovery that we are not only completely entangled with the world around us, but also that we have access to the other dimensions of who we are as well. There is no separation between people and things, and while quantum physics tells us we are all part of the fabric of the cosmos, there is a spiritual energy that completely confirms it.

Many years ago, one of my clients traveled to what was seen as a past-life experience, in which he was a young medicine man in a Native American tribe. As part of his healing work, he would move across the landscape of the battlefield between the Native Americans and the white men and help release the souls who remained close to their bodies after death following the trauma of battle. Through his own gift of seeing energy, he could see those souls rising from what he offered. As he approached a cavalry officer who lay dying, the gentle intentions of this young healer were misinterpreted. With a final burst of strength, the officer raised his pistol and shot him dead.

As all this unfolded, I asked my client, "What happens now?"

He replied, "I'm on my way to a big gathering. We become energy that feeds the trees and gives back to the earth. It is my job to see them over ... to help release them on the battlefield. A white man doesn't understand this, and he shoots me ... and now we all go up together."

While this client came to me many years ago in the early part of my career, I remember him as if it were yesterday. He was a project manager in the building industry, and at the time I was a recently "reformed" banking executive. Two males in the gentle oneness of how we can all be if we choose to. As this story unfolded and he described so simply and eloquently in a deep state of trance the beauty of this oneness, tears filled both our eyes and rolled down our cheeks.

So this external entanglement echoes inside us as our intanglement. We are intricately and intimately connected to our other selves. This in turn embraces our everywhereness, our ability to be everywhere we need to in our personal universe. This heralds the possibilities of the quantum consciousness experience. Beyond our imagination everything is possible.

This in turn empowers our creator effect, which then grants us through our own intention the ability to manifest that which we seek, to move to that higher vibration and to transcend the energy of a difficult world. To be in this world, without carrying the energy of this world. To move from the shadows and be the beacon of light that we already are, though we may have forgotten. Then, finally, to know that our journey of healing or discovery ripples out into the collective. It ripples through our other selves first of all by creating that intention. Then it raises the vibration of those we care for and are more closely entangled with, in turn enriching the collective consciousness of humanity.

If we change ourselves, we can change our planet. If we change our planet, we can raise the vibration of the universe itself. This is the simple phenomenon of holographic healing.

Surely this is an intention that can draw humanity together toward a greater purpose. Our earth is a living and breathing entity, and we are the cellular community of her innermost structure. We can be her health or we can be her disease. The choice is ours.

At the time of writing, the quantum consciousness experience has been offered by the accredited facilitators of the Institute for Quantum Consciousness for around the past five years. We started to experiment with the techniques in 2012, finalized the models and commenced trainings in 2013, and have made other refinements since.

We founded the Institute for Quantum Consciousness in 2014 with the intentions for further consciousness research, the training and support of quantum consciousness facilitators, and the offering of these experiences by a network of accredited facilitators. The institute and all we undertake are underpinned by the values of integrity, wisdom, authenticity, and inspiration. Our public launch of this remarkable experience was made at the Australian Afterlife Explorers Conference in January 2015 in Sydney, Australia. At that time, we had compiled something like one hundred case-study experiences that gave us some early evidence of trends and a flotilla of individual stories to draw upon and share with the assembled group. The number of cases has reached five hundred and expands even more through our network of facilitators who offer these experiences in their practices.

By the time you read this book, our work will have evolved even further. At this time, let us take a journey through the conceptual framework of a session and some of the experiences.

The quantum consciousness experience is offered by a facilitator who has been trained, coached, and accredited by our institute. We know that following the publication of this book, many people will experiment with these techniques, and while consciousness and the quantum realm are part of who we all are, we can only vouch for those we know and have trained. A list of these people can be found at www.instituteforquantum consciousness.com/accredited-facilitators, and they come from all walks of life, having already been trained as health or energy practitioners before being drawn to this amazing work.

The quantum consciousness facilitator will spend a little time chatting about the intention for the experience and the journey through the client's personal universe. Perhaps there is a particular reason to undertake a session or something in life that yearns for an expanded or collective view. Ultimately, the quantum consciousness facilitator will refine or expand that intention so that the full potential of the journey may be embraced. With a few deep breaths and some relaxation, the journey commences, and we embark upon the change to the present consciousness and the underlying mindsets. We embrace a quantum perspective through a series of phrases offered through a specific intention of the facilitator.

We call this the *guidance,* and the carefully selected phrases echo a Remembering of the possibilities held in the subatomic particles of the client, honoring both the individual uniqueness of that client and the greater connection to all there is in a profound and holographic way.

These are some further examples of what we say to the client to create the energy of the experience:

- "As we journey through the expanding realms of consciousness, we release the beliefs that bind our thoughts
to current consciousness thinking and all unconscious
behaviors and attitudes that keep us grounded and connected to this physical realm. As we do that now, you are
free to experience your own personal universe, unfolding
before you in all its magnificence."

- "Today we carry the intention to send an instantaneous
wave of evolving consciousness, rippling through our holographic universe into all there is."

- "We are more than a mystic collection of subatomic particles ... In a quantum world, things are not as they seem.
We can explore both this and any other reality ... all for
the greater purpose, expansion, and evolution of (client
name)."

- "In this moment, we now transcend time and space as we
know it, embracing a world where the past, present, and
future exist in perfect unison."

- "We are part of an ever-expanding universe, and we surrender to this sacred and naturally unfolding journey ..."

Following the creation of this sacred space between facilitator and client, we start the journey out through the realms of
consciousness. These will be covered shortly as I move through
them in detail and then share the stories of some of the journeys
of the institute's clients.

Ultimately, the words of the guidance we offer go beyond
these examples above and, in alignment with the sacred intentions we hold as quantum consciousness facilitators, activate

something greater than all of us under the purest of intentions. We simply bring into our connection between client and facilitator an energy that transcends the heaviness of what we encounter in our world. It could be said that this is an energy created by those higher intentions held by a facilitator who works with the energy emerging from the potential of a client's personal universe. Their belief in the client's potential is paramount. It could also be said that this is a new energy offered to a troubled world by other beings that care greatly for the future of humanity.

Perhaps it is a combination of both. I do know that we are at our most powerful when we enroll in something greater than ourselves. That's when we transcend the restrictions of the human condition and move beyond what we believe ourselves to be. This is one of the core intentions of the quantum consciousness experience and one of the leading mindsets that evolve the knowing of the present consciousness, in preparation for the unfolding journey through your personal universe.

5
THE REALM OF STORED CONSCIOUSNESS

We store energy within us and around us that reflects everything that has happened in our lives. In linear time, we may see this as our past history, present moment, and future happenings. When I created the modality of Hypnoenergetics, I embraced the simple principle that every event in our lives creates energy. This energy is the connection between an event that creates a feeling and then is anchored by a belief. This triangular relationship embedded deep in the subconscious energy field underpins our overall reactions, behaviors, moods, and choices in life. We have millions of these triangles stored in our energy field, and they hold our greatest traumas and deepest potential, and we decide how this energy is stored through our own (sometimes even unnoticed) free will.

When we visit the realm of stored consciousness in a quantum fashion, we become all about the possibilities outside of time

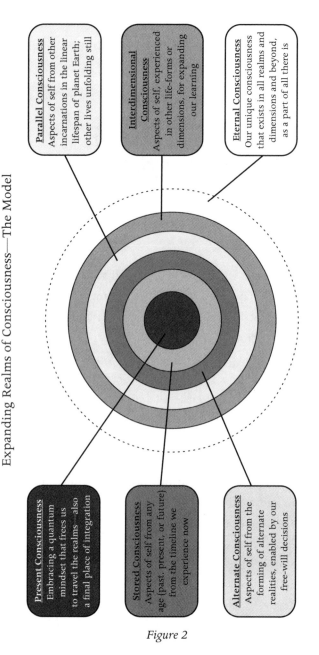

Expanding Realms of Consciousness—The Model

Parallel Consciousness
Aspects of self from other incarnations in the linear lifespan of planet Earth; other lives unfolding still

Interdimensional Consciousness
Aspects of self, experienced in other life-forms or dimensions, for expanding our learning

Eternal Consciousness
Our unique consciousness that exists in all realms and dimensions and beyond, as a part of all there is

Present Consciousness
Embracing a quantum mindset that frees us to travel the realms—also a final place of integration

Stored Consciousness
Aspects of self from any age (past, present, or future) from the timeline we experience now

Alternate Consciousness
Aspects of self from the forming of alternate realities, enabled by our free-will decisions

"All There Is"

Figure 2

and space. The higher vibrations we seek on this journey no longer reflect these old experiences as the traumas they may be but as possibilities for healing and exploration in a space of timelessness, which means we are able to access ourselves at any age.

In stored consciousness, we are looking at ourselves as we are, have been, or will be, before we move out through the other realms to other realities, parallel lives, or dimensions. Quantum consciousness facilitators ask to interact with those who have healing to seek or wisdom to share: "And as we expand out through the stored consciousness of this lifetime, we have access to all times and places that we have or will experience in this lifetime we currently know. We ask now for any ages to come forward who have wisdom to share for our journey or require healing energy to become whole."

Case 1: Sarah's Fears

Sarah, at age forty-two, found herself at a crossroads. She had resigned from a full-time and safe job in order to pursue her dream of becoming a writer and speaker, helping people heal themselves. She was dealing with the fears associated with this transition and wanted to embrace the trust to follow that dream.

As Sarah entered her realm of stored consciousness, she saw various aspects of herself, including her child self and an older self. The first Sarah who stepped forward was twenty-seven. She was very happy and told Sarah that her decision to marry was the correct one as it allowed her to be who she is. This union offered her such strength, and she could feel the bond between her and her husband. Young Sarah told her to let go of the doubt and accept the love and strength that is so strong around her. This wisdom helped her defeat fear, knowing she doesn't have to face this on her own.

It was that unconditional love that offered strength, and Sarah shared it with a young child version of herself, who appeared timid, scared, and vulnerable. The next interactions between them unfolded in the most beautiful way: "I see so clearly to tell her that love is within. She is looking for love everywhere, doing things she doesn't have to do to get others to love her. Trying and trying, seeking love—she doesn't need to feel like that. If she looks within, it is there! We all come with that gift; I'm just showing her. Putting light into her heart, so bright...She is so bright."

Sarah was able to share the unconditional love she had found with the child her, and then, finally, an older version of Sarah came forward. She was weak and dying, though she had no regrets and was so peaceful and very happy. When she showed this to the child Sarah, the child smiled brightly and ran off to play. The older Sarah had a message: "Love is within. It is your core, and stay true to that very essence." The older Sarah kissed present Sarah and was gone. Sarah's journey continued to expand through the other realms of her personal universe.

Sarah's case is typical of the interactions we see in the realm of stored consciousness. It is common to see a child come forward and learn from the other aspects of the self. The reassurance of the twenty-seven-year-old and the wisdom of an aging and fulfilled Sarah played a role in a deeply moving experience in which the client found everything she needed within her personal universe and her other selves. We often see a moving experience in this first realm as an indication that the realms that follow will be even more powerful as we take the resources gained with us further on the journey.

Case 2: Paul's Leap of Faith

As an alternate health practitioner, Paul felt a deep pull toward helping people overcome the emotional blockages in their lives. Over the years his work had expanded to the point where he wondered what to do next. He was teaching and writing articles, though something was holding him back. At one of our trainings, Paul courageously asked to be the demonstration in front of a class and journey through the realms of consciousness with the support of a loving and understanding group in attendance.

Paul moved easily into his expanded state as the others watched and held him in loving space. As he gently drifted into the realm of stored consciousness, Paul was a little surprised when his eight-year-old self came forward to greet him. Little Paul took his hand, and his present self was instantly transported to a public pool, where they stood on the diving blocks together, looking down and remembering a feeling of trepidation. Little Paul explained that you simply have to jump, and it's that simple. Just decide and act.

The wisdom of little Paul was so powerful. Paul realized at that moment the extent of the procrastination he had been creating. They held hands and jumped together, and Paul's energy changed in an instant as the jump was completed. Through the eyes of a child, Paul learned about courage, and from that moment everything changed. So often in our deeper transformational experiences, we see a child who needs healing, though in the lighter energy of the expanded states experienced in quantum consciousness, we often find the child to be the teacher.

Following this session, Paul, drawing on the new energy of certainty, had the courage to send a manuscript he had been writing to a publisher. It was accepted, and he became a published author in his field.

Case 3: Pete's Sixty-Year-Old Self

The final case in this section is one of my own. Ultimately, the understanding of this work has come in part from my own personal experiences of my own realms as a client and is really a great source of my passion and belief in the quantum consciousness experience.

As this work started to emerge, we could already see the potential of how this could serve people in this time of need. At the time of its emergence, I already had a number of roles in life. I was leading the Hypnoenergetics work, and we were training practitioners through a 600-hour course. I was also president of the Newton Institute, serving in a volunteer capacity with a staff of 60 volunteers and a network of 220 practitioners in 40 countries. This formal not-for-profit organization took up a large part of my time. In addition to all that, I had my own busy clinical practice in the eastern suburbs of Melbourne. There was little room for quantum consciousness, whether it be the design, experimentation, research, or the writing of the book you are currently reading.

With this on my mind, I entered my realms under Melina's gentle and loving facilitation. In the stored consciousness, two aspects of myself came forward. I was fifty years old at the time of this particular experience, and the first who came forward was my fifty-five-year-old self. He was weary beyond measure, tired and frustrated. He told me that he had tried to do it all— he had continued to lead the Hypnoenergetics modality and its trainings, continued to oversee the Newton Institute, and tried to start the quantum consciousness movement. None of this was as successful as it could be. He told me that spreading himself so thin had led him to burnout, disenchantment, and a mindset where he felt sorry for himself, wondering where it all went wrong. We spent time in a way that allowed him to release all that had occurred in his experiences, and the act of sharing that with someone who understood him so well was healing for him. When our interactions were complete, he felt better, and I was forewarned about a possible path I was considering.

The next person who stepped forward was my sixty-year-old self. The first impression was of sparkling blue eyes and a sense of serenity surrounding him. I basked for a moment in his peaceful energy, his humor, and the energy of the gentle wisdom he offered. His hair was completely white, and he sported a ponytail, a little different from my style and coloring of hair now, though it offered a gentle acknowledgment of how far he had come in the intervening ten years. He told me to let go. He told me I couldn't do it all and that I had to be free of the things that may hold me back from my own potential. He told me of his passion for the work and how to follow the path of least resistance, to get into the flow and allow what should naturally occur ... to occur.

As I looked deeply into his eyes, I could see the need to believe in the work and follow my own advice: the absolute surrendering to a greater energy could lead to fulfilment and purpose in ways I hadn't yet found. I sensed I could trust his judgment.

Following this experience, I retired from teaching the four dimensions of Hypnoenergetics while the rest of this remarkable quantum consciousness work emerged. (Four years later, "Hypnoenergetics—The Fifth Dimension" was to emerge as a pathway toward quantum consciousness.)

I also changed my clinical practice to shorten my working week so I had time for the reading, research, and experimentation of quantum consciousness in partnership with Melina. The space we created allowed for the founding of our Institute for Quantum Consciousness.

The door to my sixty-year-old self has stayed open. He sometimes imparts further guidance, and I feel him around in crucial moments. I even felt him intervene when I was about to make a bad business decision, and again I followed his advice. I was really surprised to suddenly hear a voice yelling in my ear, during a business meeting, with a firm and unshakeable warning!

The beauty of these interactions, this wisdom, this guidance, is that it can be made available to all of us. And we are still just at the first realm in our journey ...

6
THE REALM OF
ALTERNATE CONSCIOUSNESS

There are many theories of alternate realities and how and why they form. A quantum view embraces the theory that it comes down to choices we make, in which we take different directions and continue these existences in unison. This may be hard to get your head around, though Hollywood has made an interesting attempt to bring some of these principles to the big screen. *Sliding Doors*, a 1998 romantic comedy starring Gwyneth Paltrow, is one such attempt that carries the concept off well: the movie flips between the two very different timelines unfolding side by side, following the lead character either missing or catching a morning train.

I offer a general theory of alternate realities that comes from the background of expanded states work and the experimentation we have completed to date. All good theories evolve, and their creators will likely have more to add or develop even an entirely different concept at some future time—such is the evolving nature of this work.

Quantum physics embraces the concept of the multiple worlds theory. Those conversations started back in 1957 with physicist Hugh Everett's doctoral thesis, back then called his *relative-state formulation*.[26] This can be easily researched if you are interested; however, in a nutshell, Everett proposed that rather than the observer collapsing the wave function and forcing the subatomic particles to be in an observed state, they continue on and exist in all different possibilities in an unlimited number of universes that keep expanding.

While this is a remarkable underlying concept that stretches even the strongest intellect, I feel one of the critical factors in human existence has been forgotten and one that all spiritual people hold as a different and an even more powerful foundationary concept. We have a soul.

If we start at this point and work back toward quantum principles, we can blend these concepts together. I pondered this theory for a long time with regard to toast. If I'm deciding to have jam or honey on my toast, does this create two separate realities where I am eating my breakfast? What would be the catalyst for this remarkable toast-driven quantum event that creates a whole extra realm just because I had jam? Then we can ask, what if I forgot to go to the store and buy the honey, or, worse still, if I decide next day to have both honey and jam on the same piece of toast? Does this lead to a collision of separate universes at the cost of billions of lives? Forgive my humor

---

26. Also referred to by Brian Greene as the "Many Worlds interpretation" in *The Fabric of the Cosmos*, 205–206.

and the illogical argument that I'm deliberately building here. My point is simple, and I merely wish to share that if we start from the other end and work backward, it gets easier.

Let's go back to the soul, our immortal essence, and start there, again referencing the work of Michael Newton and his seven thousand case studies of superconscious memory obtained from clients who had access to the spiritual realm. One of Newton's key findings was the concept of the *life selection room*.[27] This is the place where we choose our bodies and the different lifetimes before we incarnate, with the view toward learning as much as we can so that our souls may evolve further. We may have up to three or more lives to choose from, and we make these selections by viewing metaphorically on a screen how each of those lives will pan out. We set up points of choice that help us to resolve karmic issues that have sometimes been with us for many lifetimes. Having facilitated many of these sessions myself over many years as a Life Between Lives hypnotherapist, I've had personal validation of these key concepts.

There are three other findings in Michael Newton's work relevant to these discussions:

1. When we incarnate, we leave some of our energy back in the spiritual realm. We decide how much to bring with us depending on the certain life we choose before we come

---

27. See chapter 12, "Life Selection," *Journey of Souls* by Newton (Llewellyn, 1994), 221–248, and chapter 9, "The Ring of Destiny," in *Destiny of Souls* by Newton (Llewellyn, 2001), 355–94.

and the challenge of sometimes doing as much as we can with a limited supply of our overall energy.[28]

2. As discussed back in chapter 2, we also know that energy can be split between two or even more bodies in order to learn more rapidly. This shows us that a soul can split energy in order to accelerate its development.[29]

3. We know that once we return and debrief a lifetime, we can energetically perform a psychodrama of the different scenarios we played out in that lifetime, even to the extent of swapping roles with other souls and seeing how events may have unfolded from making different choices.[30]

So as we set up these lifetimes, how deeply can we go into them before we make that choice? Do we perceive all the possibilities available to us? Do we see the forks in the road that then allow us at an even deeper level to know the full potentials of individual choices?

For most clients, this is an interesting aspect, though it is often not the prime focus of their LBL, as they seek the answer to bigger questions, such as their purpose for this lifetime and why they returned here.

However, I had one client give one of the most detailed descriptions of her selection possibilities. The following conversation comes from my client Robyn as she viewed the possibilities for this life before she incarnated. The transcription of our con-

28. Newton, *Destiny of Souls*, 116–124.

29. Newton, *Destiny of Souls*, 116–124.

30. Newton, *Destiny of Souls*, 164–69.

versation begins when she mentions a "hub" from which she can view parallel universes:

Robyn: It's that space where parallel universes come into a hub. There's a center point from which universes extend, everything extends, and sitting in that hub, you can see many places at once. You can see alternative outcomes, and so it's a good place to sit if you have decisions to make. You can look at where the different directions might lead you.

Peter: So you can actually peruse the choices?

Robyn: Yes. You can see them. In my case, I see them as images. Others see them in different ways, but it's a very useful space, and it's certainly accessed through this energy that can be held by Andrew and Ellen (client names her guides) and can be accessed by Robyn.

 So, it's a very good ritual to develop. It's one that needs time and developing and needs to be treated as a sacred space. So there needs to be a significant little ritual about entering it and about the gratitude for the information it provides, but it's a great space to sit and make decisions … both in the physical world and in the spirit world, because it's vast.

Peter: So this is really observing alternate realities before they occur?

Robyn: Yes, but you can see them before they form. The minute you make a decision one corridor, one reality, begins to grow a little stronger. Then, you make another decision, and that reality either strengthens as you move toward it or it wanes again as you move away toward another one.

So you are constantly shifting and realities are expanding according to each individual decision. But it's the collective decisions that really influence which track you go down. So, you might make one little decision that moves you in one direction, but if the majority of your decisions move you toward another reality, then that's where you will mainly go. But the realities literally generate and expand as you move into them. They don't exist until you make your decisions and start moving.

Peter: So they don't exist till you make your decisions?

Robyn: No, that's why it's so infinite, because they are tailored to you.

Peter: So these other ones that no longer are held in the decision, the ones that wane ...?

Robyn: They just shrink like the air going out of a balloon.

Peter: Disappear?

Robyn: For you, they do. They just shrink like the air going out of a balloon. They just collapse, and they're still available if you change your decision and want to go back. It's only the one that you're in that's fully expanded at any one time, but from any point within that expanded reality, you can shift to another simply by making new decisions ... new sets of decisions and new attitudes. Then what was a fully expanded existence begins to collapse, and the one you are moving toward now begins to expand. So it's very fluid. Every life is a very fluid, infinite existence.

Peter: So these are the decisions that you make within a life?

Robyn: Yes.

Peter: And every different incarnation holds these?

Robyn: Yes, that's right, and then in spirit you can review them. But you still ... I guess it's fair to say we all have a tendency both in spirit and in the physical realms to move into particular areas. We have areas where we feel comfortable, so our realities will tend to have a bias to them. We'll tend to be biased toward certain directions but we're not fixed in those. If at a later time we are no longer attracted to a particular area of activity or work or knowledge, or if another one sparks our interest and we wish to explore that, then we can shift and change.

Peter: So it's like we follow the energy of our intuition?

Robyn: Yes, we follow, and that shows up as our passion, what sparks our interest. I guess our passion is in the physical, what makes us go, "Wow, I'd like to know more about that!"

That's a sign that our intuition is biasing us in that direction. But we can hold multiple realities at once. We can have many aspects even in the physical, where we, for example, may be a teacher by day and a musician and a family person and be involved in hobbies and sporting groups. So each of those has its own expanded reality that increases as we are consciously aware of it, then reduces as we move into another one. We can have multiple realities happening at once, even in the physical where we have limited ability ... but of course in spirit we can expand that colossally, because we are not limited by human understanding.

Peter: So you could, if you like, live in a number of different universes at once ... in spirit?

Robyn: Yes, definitely, and if we were able to carry some of that capacity into the physical body, we could live two or three or a dozen physical lives at once. And if we could carry enough capacity, we would be able to be aware of those lives. We could be conscious in the human sphere of what the other lives in that sphere were also doing, although they may never meet and they may be on opposite corners of the earth. But the beings that do that are rare. That's a very advanced training to carry that sort of capacity into the human realm.

Peter: This ability to move between realities in human form and to help with the decision making of all these things ... how is

this helpful to humanity? How could this be used in a healing sense?

Robyn: Because the system is tailored to individual needs, it
can be dot-point specific, it can pinpoint areas of a human
life that need support or clearing energy-wise. It can look
at broader systems. It could be used to access areas of the
whole planet or the wider universe, where there are, again,
energy blockages. Where the energy isn't flowing as it is intended to and is potentially causing disease.

Peter: In the individual or ...?

Robyn: It could be in the individual or it could be in a very, very
broad sense—the whole planet or an ecosystem. It could be
as small or as wide as you are able to imagine its uses.

So this space entering this hub for seeing alternate realities is a wonderful way of correcting or choosing a path that
will try to correct things. Then, with that knowledge, go back
and work the energy to achieve that correction. So it needs
both: it needs the big-vision picture to see where the problem
is, and it needs the ability to distribute and redistribute energies to solve the problem. So, one gains knowledge and the
other activates that knowledge. I'm seeing a triangle, I'm seeing a being ... a spirit, probably ... because it needs somebody
of that freedom to know. Then I'm seeing the understanding
of the problem, which comes from the hub of realities, and
then I'm seeing the energy work, which may be done by the
person who sees or may be done by others under guidance,

to correct the problems. So there's a really strong triangular association there.

Those of us who work in this field understand that there are occasions when a client arrives and turns out to be a channel for greater wisdom or insight for the therapist. Often, they will turn up in some form of divine timing, even when you are researching a theory. It is like they are guided by a greater knowing, with that energy, whatever it may be, holding the intention to share sacred wisdom for the evolution of anyone who wants to hear the message offered.

Robyn's experience, while unique and in her own words, heralds a view that we set up a landscape within a lifetime where our choices bring new existences that all unfold in unison. Ultimately, this also brings a potential further splitting of soul energy, though this is a whole other area of research that requires more rigor before assumptions can be made. We need to also understand the limitations of the human intellect when trying to comprehend things that unfold, unbound by time, space, and the restrictions of human form. Ultimately, these experiences need to be "integratable," and I do indeed believe that this is the intention of our soul in bringing these experiences to us.

As I reconnected with Robyn to discuss the inclusion of her case in this book, she told me that this experience in the hub of realities has forever changed the way she makes decisions in life now that she carries this expanded perspective. That in itself is the real and wondrous reason why we would undertake these deeper journeys.

Another baffling part of all of this is how any experiment or research could ever be wrong. Perhaps when we invoke our creator effect, we may in fact manifest precisely what we want to see anyway, given we live in a universe of possibilities. There are echoes here of the famous double-slit experiment. How do particles and waves of possibility unfold? Exactly as we expect them to, as we collapse the wave function into our specific human intention.

Let's return to the toast scenario again. Would an immortal soul be compliant in the forming of two toast realities, one for honey and one for jam? We understand from the experiences of Michael Newton and others that the soul incarnated with the specific intention to evolve. A soul may indeed split energy further at one of these crossroads, as per Robyn's description in the hub where universes meet. Perhaps we can assume that the soul will willingly move into two realities because these two paths give way to different and diverse learning paths for the soul. Would the toast scenario provide this dual evolutionary path for the soul? We could assume not, on the basis that the soul would not choose to split for such a trivial decision point.

Let's pause for breath, as this requires careful consideration.

There is a theory emerging here that if we bring the "soul's intention to evolve" into the mix of alternate realities and connect it back to prelife planning, we hit a whole new integrated theory about when the subatomic particles in human form move into a scenario that "remembers" the prelife planning, and we activate the ultimate creator effect to form two new realities. This remembering is the threshold at which the subatomic particles decide to split in two directions, continuing in unison, though blissfully ignorant of each other.

But, wait—it gets even better. That split means that the two directions formed from the same collection of subatomic particles. Those particles remain entangled, and given they are still in that ever-connected relationship, we can call them forward as part of our exploration through our realms of consciousness. We can meet our other selves, those who look much like us though come from a different path, brought forward in our intention to share healing or wisdom.

Through our experimentation of this approach and again during the experiences of clients in clinical practice, quantum consciousness facilitators have seen validation of this phenomenon. In fact, these *doppelgängers*, as they are known in quantum terms, have proven easier to access than what we have seen previously in past life sessions. It is as though they continue on with their lives, just beyond the veil in that other reality. We assume this stronger connection comes from the entanglement still intact, given they once shared the same reality prior to the two separate ones forming.

Is this a robust model of alternate realities forming that would stand up to scientific scrutiny? Is this the result of our own mass creator effect, where we simply reproduce life-changing experiences because we believe that we can? Ultimately, none of this matters as much as the changes that people are experiencing from the amazing journeys into their personal universes.

One aspect of the realm of alternate consciousness is that we have been able to isolate this particular aspect of the quantum consciousness experience to target a specific decision point in a client's linear timeline. We can choose to target the feelings of regret or the desire to know "what if?" from various times in our lives. These have led to the experiences of some amazing life-changing sessions for the clients, whether they visited a scenario as part of their journey through their realms or from something they specifically wished to explore.

This next case is one in which we targeted a particular issue that had been impacting the client for a long time.

Case 4: Clare's Long-Term Guilt

For something like thirty years, Clare had held guilt from a decision made during her twenties. Back then, she had planned to marry a man, and as their wedding day grew closer, she had been having doubts. Clare had long-term feelings for another, and her heart was torn in two. From all over the country, the two families assembled in preparation for the wedding day, but in a moment of blinding passion and deep love, Clare decided to run away with her true love. They donned their backpacks and disappeared. Ultimately, they settled in another country and brought two beautiful young men into the world. At the time of Clare's session, that marriage had ended amicably, and her boys had grown to manhood. Regardless of the time that had passed, Clare's guilt from that wedding decision decades ago was still so prominent in her life.

During this session, which I facilitated, Clare and I moved down a river of energy to a place where we could meet with the other Clare who had gone through with that marriage back in her twenties. She appeared before Clare, deep in the sadness of a marriage that had never served her. She was childless, broken, and old before her time. As the two of them came together with the intention for their combined healing, something beautiful happened. Two weeks after the session, Clare wrote of her experiences in an email to me:

> It's hard to explain to someone that you met yourself down a path of a life choice you didn't make—an alternate reality—and you feel a total connection with yourself on the other path. You are two different energy occurrences but the same soul energy. There aren't words to describe this without sounding bona fide loony...I met myself as a very old, bent-over, lonely woman who was childless. I released her of her sadness by introducing her to my children, and she in turn released me from my guilt. I had made the right choice.
>
> There is something different about QC sessions. It's as if they take place in a different frequency, vibration, or level of consciousness. They feel direct. I cannot qualify what direct means. Time folds in on itself and around itself. You are there and here at the same time. In the session, the little old lady was waiting for me to come and release her sadness. She told me she knew I'd come.
>
> Releasing stuff is very quick and without the level of trauma that other forms of therapy can make a client reexperience. There was no entangled way of removing the guilt—it just was not there anymore. Like a magic trick. Now you see it. Now you don't.

It has been just over two weeks since my session, and still I find no trace of that guilt within my energy field. I don't punish myself, and I value myself more.

Clare's session is typical of the healing we often receive as part of these sessions. It is like we carry that energy of higher intention to serve the various selves we find in our personal universe. It is as though we remain in a transcended energy that rises above the trauma of the human condition and the heavy emotions that weigh us down. Clare's deep and profound experience was instrumental in her enrollment in this work, and she now offers these experiences to other people.

Further Insights into Alternate Consciousness

We have found that when we undertake the alternate reality work as a dedicated experience, there is something like a *quantum echo* that comes from the other to us. These are the times that we may choose to work with this echo as a portal toward that place of distress, rather than the full expanding realms of consciousness journey through one's personal universe. It's as though the deeper aspect of us just wants specific healing for another version of ourselves, rather than the amazing fulfilment of exploring every realm of our consciousness. Every client experience is different and becomes its own spiritual masterpiece, emerging under the sacred intention of the facilitator. We simply offer what is needed at any time. We have seen people expand from their present consciousness out through their realms to claim incredible wisdom and insight. We have seen people follow the quantum echo that takes them to a certain alternate consciousness or even parallel consciousness (covered in chapter 7). We have seen sessions that follow no rules or models and leave behind every human intention, to expand into the experience the client most needs at the time.

Our alternate consciousness carries all the free-will choices that we have made. My own personal experiences of this have been profound, as we continue to champion this work and take it further. As mentioned before, I regularly tap into my wise sixty-year-old self (I've christened him "Sixty-Pete"), and I've also arrived in an alternate reality, where in a deep depression I had moved to a life of drug-taking to lessen the pain.

I stepped into the scene where the other me was about to knowingly inject the last quantity of substance that would take his life. I took the syringe from his hand and helped him through his pain and withdrawal, which unfolded over many weeks in a space of *no-time* for me while I lay on the bed connected to his reality and in the safe hands of Melina as my facilitator. He didn't really recognize me as we spent time together in his healing haze, and I stayed till he was strong enough to be back on track.

Ultimately, in that reality, he became a novelist. I saw him at a book signing in his midsixties in London, and I saw myself join the queue to have a copy of his book signed by him. He simply wrote in my book "Thank you," turned to the person next to him acting as cashier, and said, "No charge for him."

The following case again is an example of following a specific energy that was coming to a client. This energy was one of wondering … "Did I make the right decision?"

Case 5: Richi's Other Career

Richi is to this day a talented entertainer. As one of the leading DJs in his field, he found at an early age that he could create nightclub experiences that were both popular and profitable. His unique style of music created incredible energy, and in collaboration with his business partner, he had the world at his feet. The future looked amazing, and while Richi was formally educated in other fields, it was the world of music that drew him into his passion.

Around this time, Richi saw a holy man whom he and his family had respected for a long time and who had provided guidance to Richi on other occasions. This man had an important message for Richi that would change his life: he needed to give up the nightclub scene, or it would end very badly for him. While Richi was shocked, he reflected and reluctantly followed the advice he was given. As he told others of his decision, he was met with both surprise and bewilderment.

Richi had always wondered what he had lost, and while his career had kept him connected to his music, he had turned to performing at other functions instead of nightclubs. He had forgone the glamour for a more peaceful life, though he could feel something coming to him from afar, from another place, possibly another reality. There was a sense of regret or pain or both.

Richi had extensive experience in expanded states of awareness, and as I facilitated, we followed the energy he was feeling into the reality where he had not followed the advice of the holy man. Richi arrived at the side of a hospital bed looking down at a younger version of himself. He was choked up with the distress and sadness for his other self, as this man was dying. The nightclub scene had carried a darker energy and intention, and as a result, his life was about to end. Richi was able to comfort his younger self and hold his hand as he passed into spirit, and at that time a great sadness and grief emerged from the older Richi and was released.

The powerful emotions experienced in this session were enormous, and a huge weight was lifted from the Richi in our reality. This was far too powerful to be put down to imagination, and this session, which happened in the early days of the quantum consciousness work, was instrumental in us at the Institute for Quantum Consciousness starting to understand the power of these experiences.

Richi now lives his life without regret, knowing that had he ignored the advice of the holy man, he would not be alive today. He now knows that the advice offered and his decision to follow it saved his life.

The change in Richi in regard to his music was also remarkable, as just a few months after his session, he stepped further into his power and finished recording his first album, as long-held blocks were dissolved.

Case 6: Annette's Time to Soar

Annette came for her quantum consciousness session initially out of curiosity. During the intake with her facilitator, it became apparent that there were some very shaping decisions made at ages nineteen and thirty-three that may emerge when reaching the realm of alternate consciousness.

At nineteen, Annette had broken up with a man and later discovered she was pregnant. She made the heart-wrenching decision to terminate the pregnancy.

At thirty-three, Annette made the decision to leave her marriage to the father of her three children and since that time had felt the guilt of that decision.

Given the emotional charge associated with both these events, the facilitator invited both these alternate Annettes to come forward if they had something to share. They both accepted those invitations. Healing momentum had already commenced in the realm of stored consciousness, as Annette met her seventeen-year-old, twenty-one-year old, and thirty-three-year-old selves, sharing themes of being afraid, alone, or scared. Each of them had found strength and, in the case of her twenty-one-year-old self, had found herself to be "dancing free." Already, beautiful healing had emerged, powered by the client's own resources discovered as the journey unfolded.

In the realm of alternate consciousness, the first to come forward was Annette's thirty-five-year-old self in the reality where she had stayed in her marriage. She looked fifty-five, felt sad and unappreciated, and described herself as a "doormat." When asked what she wanted to offer to her, our Annette from this reality chose to take this other Annette to a mirror, where they could merge and her other self could feel the strength she had shown by leaving her husband. The sharing of this energy brought such strength and transformation to her other self. Annette then gave her alternate two crystals, an amethyst and a rose quartz, to connect to. She described that she "could now soar, and from then on she would be able to fly."

Annette was then joined by a tall, slim, attractive woman who felt so very alone. This was the alternate her who had decided to keep the baby. The baby had passed at three months, and this version of Annette had turned to drugs and fled overseas, having not being able to hold down a relationship. She had continued to grieve for both the child and the child's father. The baby suddenly appeared and merged into this alternate Annette, showing her that she was always with her. Annette has now come to know also that the soul of this child from many years ago had returned to her as her middle child. This other version of Annette now no longer felt alone and was free. She described herself as wanting "to jump from star to star!"

Annette's story is a wonderful example of how, in the space of just a few minutes, energies that have been with us for decades can be released. Our Annette was so empowered as she helped her alternate selves, feeling so wonderfully validated for the courage she had shown with the decisions she had made and relieved at the outcomes shown to her in the other realities.

So often we feel the regret or guilt from a tough decision in life, though we neglect to remember the courage that we showed at that time. To then share that courage with our other selves not only serves to heal and be of service to them, but it also helps us understand the amazing resources we built during those difficult experiences.

The metaphysical knowing that Annette's child had returned to her as her middle child was yet another layer of this healing. It is not uncommon for this to happen, though there will be a different agreement between mother and child in this new soul contract that extends and evolves their journey together through this sacred reunion.

These last two cases of Richi and Annette offer a deeper level of peace and release from the bigger view of some of life's tough decisions. Richi's experience in particular was a great example of the quantum echo mentioned earlier. It is like he responded to another him, who had consciously or unconsciously sent a message of distress out into his personal universe from his end. Richi responded and released the distress for both of them, bringing immense comfort to his other self.

As mentioned above also, just feeling into and following one of the many quantum echoes in our personal universe can be an experience within itself of deep and beautiful healing or the accumulation of sacred wisdom.

7
THE REALM OF
PARALLEL CONSCIOUSNESS

As we commence a conversation about this particular realm we have to backtrack just a little.

Let's start with reincarnation as a concept. The concept that we live more than one lifetime is a given in many of the Eastern religions and philosophies, and this is slowly making its way to the West. In 2001, a Gallup Survey run in the USA showed that 25 percent of respondents believed in reincarnation while a further 20 percent weren't sure.[30] So perhaps for just under half their population, Americans are accepting or open to the concept.

While this survey sample of just over a thousand people is small, the survey was taken some sixteen years before the writing of this book, and a whole range of articles and books have

---

30. David W. Moore, "Three in Four Americans Believe in Paranormal," Gallup News Service, June 16, 2005, https://home.sandiego.edu /~baber/logic/gallup.html.

been published since then. It is not the intention of the quantum consciousness model to prove reincarnation as a phenomenon, as those studies are already in existence. For further understanding, I'd suggest research into the work of Dr. Ian Stephenson of the University of Virginia, who undertook extensive research without the use of hypnosis, the works of Dr. Helen Wambach, or Australian psychologist Peter Ramster.

Now, some years down the track, past-life therapists abound, espousing their services to all. You can even undertake a short survey or download an app on your phone to see who you were in a previous life. Even a psychic can supposedly tune in to your akashic records and let you know who you once were. If you are drawn to explore past-life regression, again I advocate that you find an experienced and well-trained hypnotherapist to assist you on the journey through your own knowing and not through the interpretation of another. Check their credentials and make sure they are a trained therapist as well. Past-life trauma needs deep and thorough healing at times, so it is best you find your way to someone with more than just a few days training. I see a lot of people suffering the outcomes of sessions with so-called professionals, who through best intentions, naïveté, or, at worst, low self-awareness have left their client emotionally traumatized or even only partially cleared due to their insufficient therapeutic training.

If you've made it this far through this book, then I'm going to assume you are open to the concept of reincarnation. We proceed on the basis that our eternal essence lives in different times and places according to the decisions and planning we undertake outside of the physical realm. Though let's remember that time is relative—or, as Einstein told us, actually an illusion. What happens when we drop the concept of time and free our consciousness from the linear approach required to manage this physical reality? We already know that time distorts when we move into expanded states. We can lose time in hypnotic states, meditation, or even during normal sleep patterns. If we leave "time" out of this, we are left with lives in different places and apparent time frames, unfolding in parallel, which are able to be accessed during expanded states of awareness.

Many years ago, when I started to take people on past-life regression journeys into other times and places in other bodies, I noticed a few remarkable things happening.

First, they were really *there* in that moment, totally revivifying the scene and being able to answer questions, on occasion even to a level of detail that could be historically validated. The depth and richness of these experiences started me wondering about this being in the past at all. Their stories were unfolding in a way that meant we could move forward and backward in time, and the experience was fascinating for me and life-changing for the clients.

Second, the true power of the work came when we crossed over into spirit, outside of time and space and beyond the restrictions of the physical body. As we claimed the lessons and learnings from a higher place, I found and then taught other hypnotherapists that we could uncover a recurring theme and, in true Gestalt fashion, facilitate a release across many lives at once. We could call these separate selves forward to be part of a healing ceremony and then send them back to their own times and places in a way that embraced the healed state.

So was this a figment of the imagination, or are we sending healing across time and space and even repairing a small piece of personal history? What could be the potential for the ripple effect of such a phenomenon?

In the quantum consciousness realm of *parallel consciousness*, we have come to understand that our consciousness is active in many apparent times and places on this planet, all unfolding in unison. From this comes incredible potential to heal anything required in the lineage of our soul, or even the opportunity to explore the talents and skills collected along the way of our soul's journey. While our alternates can help to guide us toward healing or wisdom from the decisions we have made along the timeline we know best, through the parallel consciousness, we ask for any other lifetime on this planet to come forward.

There is a remarkable expansion in the methodology as we move into this realm. Let's remember that all these other parallel lives across time and space have their own alternate realities from the decisions they have taken in their own lifetimes. The wisdom available to us just increased exponentially, covering the lineage of the soul as well as the alternate realities within each lifetime.

And so after we undertake the entry into this realm and the expanded states we seek, the facilitator will ask for those who have something to share to come forward:

And now as we expand further on this journey through your personal universe ... we know there have been times when the greater consciousness of who you are has chosen other lifetimes and physical bodies in order to learn, grow, and evolve through the myriad of opportunities available on this planet. All these lives continue to unfold, in parallel with this one we know best, outside the realms of time and space.

We seek now the exchange of wisdom, or the offering of healing, all with the greater evolution of (client name) in mind. We ask any of those others to come forward now and spend time with us.

Take a moment or two and let me know when they are here...

And they do come.

Case 7: A Meeting Across Time and Space for Suzanne

Suzanne is a long-term therapist learning the quantum consciousness experience to offer to her own clients. There was no set intention for this journey out through her realms other than to be given an understanding of the power behind this work. As an accomplished practitioner of expanded states work, Suzanne was granted an experience of her parallel consciousness that brought amazing learning to both of "herselves."

It is presented to you in dialogue form, so you can see the questions the facilitator uses in order to invoke responses that hold the knowing and wisdom from the client's own resources. As Suzanne entered her parallel consciousness realm, someone answered the invitation to come forward.

Suzanne: The first impression that I get is of a young woman. Brown hair tied up under a white bonnet. Dressed in a long skirt, almost like a milkmaid look. Conservative. She has come forward. She is standing there. Hair tied up in a bun. She is just twenty-five or twenty-six years old.

Facilitator: How does her energy feel to you?

Suzanne: She is just observing me.

Facilitator: Tell me more.

Suzanne: We are just observing each other. She is not quite sure what to make of me but feels a familiarity between us.

Facilitator: Ask her to tell you her story.

Suzanne: She leads a very simple life. A husband and two children. In a time of 1817 or 1800s somewhere. It's a simple life. She is happy. She is in awe. She knows who I am, that we are one and the same. She is in awe that I am there ... Because she believes she has a simple life, I'm trying to explain to her what we are doing here, expanding consciousness. She is in awe I am there. What she is offering me is a glimpse of simplicity of life. She is happy in a contented way, but in another way she is thinking, *Wow, look at what you are doing.* She is offering me a vision of what simplicity would be. I am offering her a view of what she is capable of, somewhere else.

Facilitator: How does that simplicity serve you in your current life?

Suzanne: It's just knowing that me, my consciousness, participates in so many different scenarios. There is nothing overly exciting going on in her life. It's a nice existence. No trauma apart from daily stuff, but there are no huge traumas. I get a sense it is in America. I see wheat crops … and living on the land.

Facilitator: What do you need from her?

Suzanne: I don't need anything. It's just interesting to see a different scenario. She is intrigued we have connected. It's more an exchange of acknowledgment.

Facilitator: Is there anything that you can offer her?

Suzanne: It's like she has become aware now and realizes that she is more than what she is because she has seen me. It has her thinking.

Facilitator: How can that help her?

Suzanne: It has her thinking. Thinking about herself. We are just going to have a chat now.

(The facilitator gently holds space till Suzanne is ready to continue.)

Suzanne: I have explained. It's inconceivable to her that I am not married and that I have a life. She is amazed that I don't rely on a husband to support me or look after me. That concept has blown her away.

Facilitator: How is that going to help her knowing this?

Suzanne: It has set off a fire within her. That she can be not as reliant on him and can make her own decisions. She is already strong but does defer to her husband. She is blown away that I am my own boss.

Facilitator: Is she happy?

Suzanne: Yes, she is. We are just both grinning at each other, thinking this is cool. She is looking at my clothes and touching the fabric. I must look like an alien to her, and I am wearing pants. She finds that highly amusing. Just like a man. (Suzanne laughs).

Facilitator: Have you told her what year you are in?

Suzanne: No, but I will...She is blown away. Two hundred years in the future. She is overwhelmed now. I am reassuring her. We are hugging now. It is going to take a while for all of this to sink in. She is now aware of her abilities more than she was before. It is time for me to go.

Facilitator: Thank her for coming forward.

Suzanne's case is a great example of how wisdom can be both gentle and insightful. This meeting outside time and space helps us bridge the gaps between the different so-called time periods that exist in our personal universe. What does this mean for the other self in another body? Do they have a dream or a vision or a waking state in which they describe such an experience? As our research unfolds, perhaps we can find that type of validation, similar to the way past-life recall has been validated historically.

We can ask a more pertinent question: What is happening in your own dream states as you travel your personal universe overnight? Perhaps you are the recipient of these experiences from another you who seeks to make contact. As with all the cases so far, this was just part of the journey for Suzanne's session as she came from the previous realms and entered the next one.

Later, in chapter 10, we will track client journeys through all of their realms as individual case studies. For now, let us continue to explore the realm of parallel consciousness.

Case 8: Doreen's Message to All of Us

This is an interesting case in that it shows that a simple view of life can sometimes hold the greatest wisdom. As Doreen expanded into her parallel consciousness, she was met by a young Indigenous Australian girl. I've chosen to paraphrase the words recorded from our archives and offer them to you as the facilitator of the day offered them to our institute. Doreen explained,

A girl came forward. Looks very young; however, is in her early twenties. Part of a tribe. Wearing Aboriginal clothing, living in the wilderness. Face is painted. There is an older man, in his fifties, who is the head of the tribe. His face is painted white. They live off the land. She is carrying a spear. The spear is for protection.

Her role within the tribe is healer. She collects herbs, plants, and berries and uses them to help the tribe. When the tribe is unwell, she helps them. The healing techniques are passed down from the elders. She is currently being trained by an elder. She is in the studying phase.

All tribal members are equal. Everyone has a defined role. It is a relaxed life, a simple life. She is alone at the moment—no husband. Everything flows naturally.

Everyone within the tribe has a defined role. Children are there to remind everyone of innocence, play, and being free. Everyone has an important role to play and contributes in their own way: hunters, healers, and so on. Her role is to help heal people. A natural exchange—no payment. No one gets paid. You go where you are needed. Everyone knows their role; it is clear, and they all work together. They all play their part, and it works perfectly.

They need laws and rules so that everyone is comfortable. If someone steps out of line, they are reminded to treat all well and not bring disharmony. Ripples of your actions affect everyone within the tribe.

When asked, Doreen extrapolated out the grander picture of how modern society has moved from a cohesive energy to that of separation:

Learnings … First, a reminder that there is a place for everyone. She is still part of a tribe but a fractured tribe, as there are so many of us. We don't feel our purpose because there are too many living in their heads, striving for things that mean nothing. We need to settle down and pay more attention to our hearts. Then things will flow more.

Money separates us. We have become separated. The tribe is harmonious and energy flows. Flows with the planets, the land. There is a natural order of things.

Our tribe is the human race—disharmony, wanting … have, have, have. Television is a separation tool. Separates and eludes, puts people on other levels. It's almost evil. The way it is perceived and used makes people feel worthless. We have become divided into three levels: poor, middle class, and upper class. Makes you feel more worthy to be rich and have things. This is how we see ourselves. Take all of those things away, and we are all exactly the same—there is no separation. We create the separation.

This is a great example of the offering of a higher perspective that ripples out into a broader statement about what we are doing for our planet. It is well known that indigenous cultures have a history of living in harmony with their surroundings and having cultural norms that bring a tribe's people together rather than separate them.

In fact, in the past we have seen some indigenous cultures that offer a far greater power than we know today, as we can see in the next case.

Case 9: Melina Remembers the Energy of Great Spirit

When Melina and I first started to research these experiences in expanded states of awareness, we came to understand the important nature of the environment in which we undertook the experiences. On one occasion, Melina and I took time out to travel to a secluded place in the bush and spent several days in a yurt, feeling that the energy of that type of structure would be helpful in opening pathways to a greater consciousness. These earlier sessions both helped us refine the experience for those facilitators who came later and also showed us the incredible potential of the work.

This next case of Melina's was undertaken in the yurt and was offered to us to help us remember, even more deeply, that we have other selves in our parallel consciousness who are wise and powerful. They exist within us and can be the most wonderful ongoing resource for us, once we have remembered they are there.

As Melina entered her parallel consciousness, she was transported beyond time and space to witness a powerful version of herself.

A tall and wise woman named Shanti stood on a cliff top. She was dressed in the beautiful ancient clothing of a long-forgotten culture. She wore clothing in shades of blue and turquoise and held a tall staff. As she struck her staff onto the ground, it opened up an energy portal to Great Spirit. This energy was known as Noami and was formed from the vibration of the planet, containing all of her spirit and essence. Shanti worked to open this portal so the energy could be remembered by those who have forgotten. She also worked in unison with her soul mate during this lifetime. He was a warrior of the light, and their two energies complemented each other, combining to allow them to access an even greater, but gentle, power.

As Melina and Shanti interacted, they moved so their foreheads could touch, resting their third eyes against each other's. They blended in a way that offered telepathic communication, and Shanti told Melina not to turn away from this energy so that she too could in turn share it with others. Until this time, Melina had been feeling this energy in her life without knowing the source, feeling an awareness of a quantum echo.

Following these interactions, Melina was able to connect with Shanti as she chose to, staying in the flow of the Noami energy. She was told that more information would continue to flow as time unfolded. It had been Shanti's role in her lifetime to bring this energy through for those around her, though now it had started to flow to her other selves in parallel as well.

Summary

The case studies of Suzanne, Doreen, and Melina are very different and offer a view of the breadth and diversity of what we hold in the realm of parallel consciousness. I've spoken to many people who have had short past-life readings and explorations and have come away wondering if they made things up. They have often found the experience "interesting" at best, before filing it away for an amusing chat at some time in the future. It is one thing to open a time window for a peek through, but it is another to claim wisdom, heal holographically, and serve humanity through your own deeper experiences.

I would offer to you that you have incredible wisdom held in the lineage of your soul that is still active in a quantum fashion outside of time and space. Suzanne's session showed us that even lives that appear simple help us understand the power of who we are in the present consciousness. Doreen brought through messages of a simple indigenous life that may just have the answers to some of the issues we face in the modern world in regard to separation from both others and the earth herself. Melina showed us that we have incredibly powerful lives to which we can reconnect.

There are some darker times in the history of this planet; however, we can send the light to those places, sending a ripple of healing via our other selves, who in a quantum way are still there to make a difference in their own present consciousness.

Imagine the energy we can release from the history of this planet as each of those others brings light to where they are in all times and places undertaking their own ripple effect of healing.

8
THE REALM OF INTERDIMENSIONAL CONSCIOUSNESS

As we move to this next realm, we challenge some of the prevailing mindsets even further.

Our consciousness can reside in other types of bodies, existences, and dimensions, more so than we could ever realize.

I remember as a youngster when Erich von Däniken published his book *Chariots of the Gods?* and asked the provocative question, "Was God an astronaut?"

At the time, this book and the subsequent documentary made a significant impression on me, as this man courageously challenged existing theories of whether there was life elsewhere in the universe across the billions of other planets and stars. Using archaeological findings, Von Däniken offered the unifying evidence from various ancient indigenous cultures about interactions with extraterrestrials.

In chapter 11, *The Search for Direct Communication,* Von Däniken shares the results of the Green Bank Formula, designed by a number of eminent scientists in 1961, which estimates that somewhere between forty (minimum) and fifty million (maximum) groups of intelligences are seeking to make contact with others within our Milky Way galaxy.[31] This really offers a level of objective certainty that goes beyond emotive impressions or even hypothetical opinions. It simply makes logical and practical sense that we are not alone in the universe.

As always, I needed my own proof of such a phenomenon. I was in need of certainty that I wasn't bringing some of the amazing science fiction I'd read as a youngster into fruition via conscious interference during my own expanded-states explorations. Or perhaps I was even invoking just plain-old wishful thinking.

Many years ago, as I sat in my clinic, I had a client regress into a lifetime that was a little out of the ordinary. "Tell me where you are," I said to him.

"I'm not sure. It feels very strange," replied the client.

"Allow yourself to get a sense of whether you are in a body or not, and describe what you are feeling," I prompted. (I'd discovered this request usually brought to the client a knowing of whether they were in a lifetime past or even existing as energy somewhere.) I wasn't ready for my client's reply.

"I'm about ten feet tall, and I appear to be some sort of translucent light being … I have these elongated fingers. I see others around me, and I can see straight through them."

---

31. Erich von Däniken, *Chariots of the Gods?* (London: Corgi Books, 1972), 165–67.

After allowing the session to continue bringing a level of therapeutic benefit, I brought it to a close and the client left. I considered allocating this experience to the possible "nutter" section of my files and finally categorized it as another of those strange things that happen in clinical practice from time to time.

Four weeks later, another client was taken to a lifetime in which they were "about ten feet tall." The client explained, "I feel really light. I can see through myself, and I have these really long fingers. I'm some sort of being made of light." From my side of the clinic, I was struggling just a little with thoughts along the lines of "Just my luck to get another weirdo" and "I wonder if a friend is having a joke with me."

A few more weeks went by, and another light being showed up. Now understanding that none of these people knew each other and each of them received amazing validation of themselves and deep therapeutic benefit as a result of these experiences, I conceded. I sent a message to the universe that I was now open to us all being citizens of the universe, regardless of where we have lived across the lineage of our soul.

I was then offered my own experience in my first Life Between Lives training course, held at the foot of the Rocky Mountains in Colorado. I had traveled to the United States to study LBL work with the Newton Institute.

When it became my turn to be client, I was deep in my superconscious memory, and my student facilitator asked an amazing question that I've always used since in my own client sessions: "Have you ever had a lifetime in a different type of body on another planet? If so, allow yourself to see."

I was instantly transported to the body of a dolphin-like creature, hurtling through the sea on a water world. This was shown to me so I could experience "freedom," and to this day I can remember in great detail the feeling of water rushing along my rubbery skin. This dolphin was two-tone blue with a black stripe down the side and the most stunning blue eyes, no doubt shown to me so I could see the differences from the beautiful creatures that inhabit our own world. It was an experience I'll never forget, and it gave way to bad humor in front of the rest of the class next day when I recounted the experience, claiming it had been instrumental in the discovery of "my life's porpoise."

Best we move on ...

This experience, and those of the clients who recalled lives as the light beings, was enough to remove the last aspects of arrogance and judgment from my client sessions. I become an advocate for the uncovering of my clients' truth, gently challenging human belief systems and conscious interference as needed in the interests of my clients. Though, more importantly, I started to get out of the way and allow my clients the freedom to move into their expanded states, without them having to worry about what I as their facilitator thought. I had felt the freedom as that dolphin-type creature, and now I offered that in return to all those who would come.

My experience of many hundreds of client interactions is that the vast majority of us have some form of experience as an existence in other life-forms and dimensions. This occurs as part of the lineage of our soul, if you want to consider linear time, or is currently happening in parallel in another realm of our personal universe. It is so important that as we explore this next realm, we do so in a way that releases the beliefs of a present consciousness that operates not just in linear time but from the parameters of the human condition in which we find ourselves. To facilitate this, we offer the following:

And now as we expand further on this journey through your personal universe...we know there have been times when the greater consciousness of you may have chosen existences in other forms and dimensions, in order to learn, grow, and evolve through the myriad of opportunities available in this and any other universe or dimension. All these existences continue to unfold, in parallel, outside the realms of time, space, and reality as we know it.

So we may fully experience these other existences, we now release the influences of this human form that create limitations to our deeper understanding. We embrace the new horizons being offered with complete freedom.

We seek now the exchange of wisdom, or the offering of healing, all with the greater evolution of (client name) in mind. We ask any of those others to come forward now and spend time with us...

Take a moment or two and let me know when they are here...

Of all the realms the facilitators have visited so far during the clients' journeys, this is the one that tends to stretch our beliefs beyond current knowing and into new territory.

This first case offers a wonderful example that at our core we are energy and consciousness. The greatest challenge for some of the experiences in the realm of interdimensional consciousness is for the client to be able to describe in human language what they are experiencing. The following is a summary of Philippa's experience as a golden energy form.

Case 10: Philippa's Existence as a Golden Ball of Energy

By the time Philippa arrived in the realm of interdimensional consciousness, she had already experienced profound wisdom throughout her other realms. Even moving from her parallel consciousness, where she had worked with a Maya healer aspect of herself for deeper learning about her role in healing others, had not prepared her for the existence she was about to experience.

Philippa saw herself as a collection of energy she described as a ball. She was both an individual and a collective at the same time. She described the energy as separating into millions of different aspects and then coming back into one. It was as though this collective energy was breathing, though not in a way that we know, as that did not exist in this place. Philippa really struggled with trying to describe what she was experiencing, though it eventually started to flow:

They are so alive. They are just "knowing," and they spread knowledge across the universe. One big breath and they just fly through space. Then when they need to come back, they breathe and bring back the knowledge of each individual. They share, and off they go again. They are just pure energy. The purpose of this is to watch other entities and see how they interpret the "oneness." This is another dimension, but sometimes when you see that little glint of gold in the room, that is them. When we feel that shiver go through us, it is them touching us and taking our knowledge back—it is source energy! This is the source of all energy of the universe. It compresses down to the smallest thing, into nothing, and then breathes out into everything. Tiny mass, then one big breath, and expanding out into the other galaxies. Some break off to visit other planets/galaxies; others come back. They are over all galaxies and universes. They have universal knowledge. It is infinite.

Philippa then spoke of herself in the third person. Often, we see this in expanded states, indicating that the information is coming from beyond the client's usual levels of consciousness.

This was given to Philippa today to show her that they explore how much we have grown, and that just a tiny speck of them here can gather information on that life form, go back, and share info with source. It happens constantly and continuously. Every human has this without exception. Philippa was unaware of this until now. She sees speckles of gold now and then; now she knows it is the oneness. Without this there is nothing. Philippa really enjoys this moment, these feelings...

This sounded very pleasurable according to the tone and emotion observed in the client's voice at the time.

It is the universal "breath of life." Philippa knows how to harness it; she is being reminded. It can be gifted to others. Philippa just breathes it in. Some people are better at gifting it than others—that's why we have healers. They gift it to others. We all have different skills. She has this skill that she can just draw it in: she draws it into her hands, and by touching others, she gifts it to them. She sends healing during the session. Her hands become very alive with energy. When she breathes it in, it fills the spaces between the atoms. Some understand this. Science is only now understanding it. She knew it, but she understands it now. It has to be gifted, or we become stagnant!

Now she knows what it is. Just puts her hands up and breathes it in through her body and then gifts it out. She will now give it to herself and gift it to others (not allow others to take it). Gifting will be conscious. Philippa has to gift daily so she can fill with more. It will only take minutes.

Energy gets its power from movement. Conscious gifting of energy has to happen; it has to keep moving or it loses its power.

Ultimately, Philippa's journey through her interdimensional realm has greatly changed her perspective on her healing work. She can now more "consciously" offer this energy to others in her work.

The reference to science in this case is interesting. We already know that quantum physics is starting to validate many of the old spiritual healing beliefs about universal life force energy and its application through the healing modalities.

Case 11: Nadia's Resourcefulness

As mentioned before, we observe during the quantum consciousness experience that a theme can emerge across the realms. In Nadia's case, she had undertaken her session with the aim to understand whether she is capable of having a child.

Already, she had been building resourceful energy as she moved out through her realms of consciousness. As so often happens, she was offered a very different perspective in her interdimensional consciousness.

Nadia sees herself as a large and very old squid-like creature. This existence takes place on another world. The waters around her are cool and dark, and she can feel the fragility of this world on which she is living. Her role is one of a communicator for all the species on the planet, both above and below the water. She acts as a type of satellite dish or beacon and passes messages onward without knowing what they mean, and it all happens instantaneously.

Nadia shares, "I have access to billions of bits of information. I enable species to communicate, on both land and water.

So above, so below—I am not the only one, but I am part of keeping the harmony and balance of this fragile world."

Nadia is shown that not only is she resourceful in this interdimensional consciousness she sees and feels, but she carries easily the shared responsibility for the balance it takes for a fragile world to survive. Imagine the power of seeing something of this magnitude as she pauses to reflect on whether she has what it takes to parent a child.

Already, you can see the bigger picture emerging in this realm. Once we surrender the attachment to this human form, there is incredible wisdom that awaits us in our expanded states through our interdimensional consciousness. It is starting to show us something very important. From client sessions in the interdimensional realm, facilitators often witness life-forms that do not carry the prevailing mindsets that embrace competition, separation, and fear that we carry on this planet. Perhaps the absence of such things is the natural state of all consciousness, to know that we are all connected. We are starting to prepare to see more of this as we expand further through our personal universe. This next example offers further evidence of this trend.

Case 12: Lightworkers Remembering Who They Are

Liz is a therapist, practiced in both offering and receiving expanded states experiences. The following comes from the documentation of her case as a client and is shared in her own powerful words:

We then moved to the interdimensional consciousness, and I found myself immersed in a purple light and what was beyond was enormous.

We were all beams of light radiating out colors in thin arcs and the colors were so clear, clean, pure, and crisp with an intensity of pure concentrated strength. By raising our vibration, we create this, and the colored beams create fractals. We all do this, we are all connected, and we are doing this all the time.

We create light, and this is what I am doing on earth. It's my job; I am a lightworker. The message for me was this: "She needs to remember the strength, intensity and concentration of it. There's no need to question; this is what she does. Just do it…no doubt. She needs to recognize how direct it can be, without obstacle. She allows other things to seem more important, and they are not. She had all the obstacles around her before so that she would learn to connect directly into source. She has got the connection now but has not given it the respect it deserves. She now needs to stop apologizing for who she is and use that connection. It is direct."

I was reminded that it is fun and not to take it seriously but just play and enjoy it. The wave of expanding consciousness through the realms allowed the healing to be immediate.

And as she expanded further, she added, "Remember the fabric from which we are all made, the interconnectedness of all, for although we may work from within our own energy, we are always plugged in...always connected. That energy is complete and whole, and we must work individually to allow it to be as expansive as it can be and to respect that. Respect that it can join to others, but it has to be given its full expansiveness first."

This case is a great example of how when lightworkers remember why they are here, they are then able to transcend the energy of this planet. So many times over the years I've undertaken clinical sessions for people who carry the healing vibe but have been caught up in everyday life. It is like they dove enthusiastically into the heavy energy of our planet, only to start to drown in the very energy that they came here to change.

So here is a message to all lightworkers, all healing types, all those who came here to make a difference: We know you fill many roles in the healing arts, medical systems, local communities, and businesses large and small. Underneath all the noise, you really do know who you are, and you only have to do one thing—remember who you are, remember what you are here for. When you do that, it sends a ripple into the collective consciousness of humanity. That in itself is an amazing and profound contribution to our evolution of this planet. By simply remembering, you send powerful energy out into a universe that knows how to heal holographically. When you remember, send that energy through your stored consciousness, transforming yourself at every age, and through your alternate consciousness so that all other realities can benefit from the gift you offer. Send it through your parallel consciousness so that we can change how the energy of humankind is recorded. Our parallel selves in turn can pass it to their other stored and alternate realms as well. Send it to your interdimensional consciousness experiences, and more than anything they will hear you, as connectivity and transcending this energy are what they are used to.

Summary

By now, you will start to understand the immense healing potential of these journeys as we leave restrictive mindsets behind and embrace the powerful ripple effect available through the holographic nature of existence. This is simply the natural order of the greater universe in which our consciousness resides.

A theme is also emerging about life itself. As the realms expand, we are seeing a trend toward interconnectivity of all life.

There is a real knowing that as we move further from the restrictions of this human form (please don't take that personally), we release any perceptions of separation and move into what appears to be a feeling of collective freedom.

But wait—we aren't finished yet...

9
THE REALM OF
ETERNAL CONSCIOUSNESS

There is an aspect of our consciousness that exists in every realm. We can be in the forever-changed present consciousness of who we are, and we can be in any alternate consciousness or even parallel consciousness, all still with a single unifying and unique *eternal consciousness* that records our experiences as the lineage of our soul.

We can move out through interdimensional consciousness and start to feel what it is like to exist as something other than our known human form, though again, even in that state of being our eternal consciousness is still present.

We have been gradually expanding through the realms of consciousness model to increasingly transcend the heavy energy that permeates our earth, bringing a deeper knowing to our client about who they truly are. Our intention for the realm of eternal consciousness is for the client to feel their deepest, expanded authenticity. A quantum consciousness facilitator will then offer to the client, "And now your personal universe expands to your eternal consciousness...transcending all realms and existences. This eternal state now unfolds within you and around you, connecting you to the universe itself. Feel this expanded state of being..."

Facilitators gently hold the energy of the client as they experience this aspect of their existence. Sometimes the clients share what they are experiencing, and other times it can't be described. The role of the quantum consciousness facilitator at this time is simply to be of service.

On occasion, comments are offered by clients while in this energy. Here are a few:

- "I'm vibrating all over like a crystal. I'm picking up a grid with crystals arranged in beautiful symmetry like a mandala. All the energy is together. I'm having a powerful, peaceful connection. I am a being, feeling spirit without even trying. I'm just being a spirit, letting it flow and staying on a positive level of existence. It is how it feels to be between lives, not on earth, being a little piece of a crystal in a larger grid. It is boundless expansion."

- "Millions of little cells with everything that makes me. There are lights in front of me, millions of them like a string. Where the universe is a fabric, every time consciousness occurs there is a cross formed on the string—holographic. All is there; every cross is one of me, one with the universe."

- "Floating into nothingness, where there are no thoughts, weightless, like floating in space. Life on earth is just a little speck. Don't get caught in the drama. Look for the nice times because you are only there for a short time. Enjoy it as much as possible."

- "A feeling of being enormous and tiny at the same time. Everything and nothing. Other than that, beyond words. An understanding of the infinite from a nonphysical perspective. An understanding I have experienced before while in this body but only in the dream state."
- "Wonderful waves of expansion, the vastness is amazing. Nothing matters, yet everything matters…"
- "I'm floating in darkness, and now I'm being perforated with light and energy."

Ultimately, the feelings associated with this part of the client's experience carry an energy not normally experienced in human form. This is a time of the utmost respect and consideration of the person who comes to explore their personal universe. At times, they may share, and at other times, facilitators may be guided by our intuition to ask a question, allowing the client to offer immortal insights.

In the majority of cases, we simply hold sacred silence as a way to honor the person before us. This is a moment when the remembering of who we are in our deepest authenticity allows for the experience of looking down on a troubled planet as a distant speck somewhere else in the universe.

Ultimately, all we have collected on our journey through the realms of consciousness is with us still and this offers a chance for an even greater perspective on what we have experienced thus far, offered from this eternal aspect of our self.

Sometimes to aid our integration of the experience, we are shown metaphors or meet other beings:

- "My sister who passed is waiting for me. We embrace ..."
- "I'm shown a wolf that howls at the moon. He howls 'joy' and it ripples through the woods, spreading joy everywhere."
- "My grandfather tells me everything will be okay."
- "I'm sitting in a garden, a peaceful place with so much green. I am healing."

We often see the use of metaphor and analogy offered as a way to learn when in contact with deeper states. Let's remember, the intention of the immortal spiritual aspect of ourselves is to grow and learn from experiences gained through incarnations both here and elsewhere.

In order for this to occur we need to experience something that is "integratable." This is a well-known phenomenon in Life Between Lives sessions, where the gradual unveiling of the superconscious finally takes us into another dimension, the spiritual realm. Here we encounter libraries of akashic records, gardens where we meet with soul friends, and temple-type structures where we meet with advanced beings for guidance in the current life.

This experience of feeling the eternal consciousness as part of our personal universe differs in that just for a moment we enjoy the Remembering of our expanded state without expectation or intention—a pure transcendence, far away from the present consciousness that seems to rule our lives here on earth.

Once we have felt and experienced this pure state of being, we take a further step into the expansion, as we offer our wisdom collected on the journey into all there is:

As you now experience the limitlessness of your expanded state of being ... there is a profound shift in your personal universe ... and you become an instantaneous wave of evolving consciousness ... rippling through our holographic universe ... offering your sacred contribution to the fabric of the cosmos.

You feel this wave ... returning to you ... in the form of gratitude, permeating your being ... Take a moment to feel this now.

You become one with all there is ...

Remember always, this is who you really are ...

The intention of this final aspect of the journey through your personal universe is to remember and reclaim your rightful place among the energy of all there is.

Blending completely with all there is offers us two things. First, we have a chance to feel our contribution to the evolution of the universe. Our session already underway increases the wisdom of all there is and forms our own sacred contribution to the everything, of which we are a part. Second, what we offer we then receive back in gratitude in that beautiful return ripple effect. We have offered a gift to all there is. We then receive the wisdom in return, as we are part of it too—a universal gift for what we have offered.

Again, this moment is a time to pause and hold the energy of sacred silence, somehow intuiting when to offer the words on the previous page and when to allow space for the experience.

Facilitators may continue to hold the silence that continues, though at times we are offered some beautiful words as the client does their best to encapsulate the experience in words:

- "I'm being shown how time bends and the universe folds. Consciousness moves through it. I can't put it into words."

- "I am aware that I am part of the universe and interconnected with it. I am given the words *strength*, *safe*, and *capable*, and I am asked to call back here more often."

- "I see eternity as a classroom, with millions of dots... that's us."

- "I experience the silence of creation."

- "We each carry our own universe within, and as we balance our own energy, the flow helps heal the planet and the universe we inhabit."

Imagine the shifted perspective of what we refer to as the *forever-changed present consciousness* following the quantum consciousness experience.

The integration of the experience can take time and a dedicated conversation from the quantum consciousness facilitator. Each of these experiences is rich and diverse and is worthy of its own separate and unique integration.

10

THE QUANTUM CONSCIOUSNESS EXPERIENCE

One of the characteristics of this work is that a journey out through the personal universe carries a dedicated theme through every realm that continues to evolve as the client expands, offering ever-increasing healing and perspective. These particular sessions offer something very special. They bring an alignment of all realms toward a single powerful message, which usually draws on a prominent life issue being faced or a greater need for expanded wisdom.

The final three cases are examples of following a client out through the expanding realms of consciousness model.

Case 13: Jane and the Myth of "Separation"

Jane wished to undertake the quantum consciousness experience to explore a deeper knowing that she sensed was just out of reach. She felt in her heart that the belief in separation was indeed just a collective mindset that exists in humankind and that we are all connected at a deeper level.

Jane and I, her facilitator, embarked with the intention to understand more of this theme. As we expanded the present consciousness under our philosophy of moving to the quantum mindset, Jane moved quickly into an expanded state of consciousness.

As we moved into the stored consciousness, two aspects of Jane came forward. There was an older her and a young child, though both held the same innocence and the same delight. Jane felt that they were not apart and were in fact the same. It was merely their belief in time that kept them apart. Jane remarked, "This is what no separation looks like in human form. We are the same. It is merely where you punctuate in time that sets us apart." Jane was told that this concept was important to take forward through the other realms we would visit.

As we moved into the realm of alternate consciousness, two more aspects came forward. One Jane appeared huddled and small, and the other was confident. The confident one offered that she had come to share resources that she had built in her reality, specifically strength and confidence to help the other aspect of Jane firmly plant her feet on this earth and prevail in a difficult existence. She told us that when the new ways and the old ways meet, the energy becomes unstable. The huddled and smaller Jane reflected another reality, where deep sadness had her wondering whether she wanted to stay in a difficult world. The confident Jane offered her hand, her understanding, and a promise that they would travel together from now on: "Where you go, I go." They then became one, in a beautiful unifying of their energy. We sent a ripple of healing and wisdom through this realm and beyond as we continued to expand through Jane's personal universe.

When we entered the realm of parallel consciousness, Jane found herself in front of a cloud. She put her hand into the cloud to draw out the person she needed to meet. A Native American man stepped out of the cloud, greatly honored to be invited. He offered Jane his experience of "listening to the land." What does it need and want? How can it help him? He told Jane, "In the listening, there is no separation. Even taking a step on the earth is interacting."

He then transformed into an elder at a later time in his life, sitting on the earth, breathing and listening. A part of his role was to bring in the Remembering of this knowing, to act as a bridge to this world and what was needed. He brought his forehead to Jane's, and as they both stood there for this sacred moment, she felt that they were the same. This Native American elder offered Jane a steadiness, a standing firm for the quality of the Remembering. It was now moving from "being held" to "flowing." He told Jane, "What we do has been held in place for centuries until it was ready to be added to, honoring those who have gone before." He then sent Jane an imprint of energy of the experience of standing firm in the Remembering so that she too could be in service to those in forgetfulness. Again, we sent this discovered wisdom through this realm and beyond before we expanded further.

As we entered the realm of interdimensional consciousness, Jane experienced what she described as a "pulse." Her role was to receive a vertical stream of light that comes to her, which she then converted to the pulse. Her role was to send the pulse for this sector that includes earth though echoes into other realms also. Jane explained, "It works like a ripple on a pond. The requirement of the pond is the call of Remembering. It carries the wisdom and knowing of what is required. I send it out, and if I were not here, another would come. Some hear it and pass it on. There are different vehicles for the Remembering. It connects with a core that can't be touched. There is a quality of waking up or activating, amplifying what already is, though how each responds is unique to them. There should be great peace knowing this is in place."

When asked how this pulse could be more consciously activated and shared, Jane responded, "Receive the pulse and show the way. Know much is in place. It is helpful to sit in silence and receive for self-Remembering. The pulse contains information, details of the Remembering guidance. Hearing it better amplifies the Remembering."

Jane's whole demeanor changed, reflecting a deeper wisdom, as she shared this information. It is common to receive information in the interdimensional realm that seems to surpass human understanding, though at a broad level the messages were clear. Again, as always, we sent this wisdom through this realm and beyond before we continued.

As we moved to eternal consciousness, Jane simply merged into an energy she described as "the space between the pulses." She rested there for quite a while before continuing.

As we moved out further and became part of the fabric of the cosmos, Jane spoke again, describing her experience:

"I am silence, the pause before creation...the pause of all the possibilities—the moment before. All that is created from the silence...that carries the echo that holds it together. The relevance for Remembering is silence, sending all this to those on the planet who are standing firm. See the pulse with an absence of distance from it...making a doorway...receive it with the clarity of knowing its presence. Standing firm above all else and listening for the silence."

Jane spoke further about how it is time for the "harvest." She spoke of the seeds of this Remembering that have been sown and over time have held a "steadiness and Remembering" and how this is now starting to flow out for all of us.

This first case of the flow across the realms as a theme was one of our earliest cases, and it became instrumental in the formation of some of our key themes that underpin quantum consciousness.

Jane was shown initially that time is the only separation within the self if we choose it. We are our child self and our older, wiser self, all in unison. There is no separation at this level.

Next, we were shown that we have the capacity in a powerful reality to share the resources with those realities that need them the most. As Jane's two alternate selves unified, again we saw no separation.

The Native American man showed us there is no separation between us and the earth. Then, as he became the elder, he showed that his role was to hold the wisdom and to help others remember. Again, as their foreheads touched, Jane understood that the two of them were the same.

The experience of the pulse and Jane's role in bringing that and sharing it took this alignment of all things even further. We are part of all there is, and as we continued Jane's journey, she moved into a greater connection into all there is, simply Remembering that this is who we really are.

Case 14: Melissa Releases What Holds Her Back

This next case across the realms shows an example of how a session can unfold differently at times, depending on the needs of the client and their greater evolution. Ultimately, everything happens just as it is meant to ...

Melissa came with the intention of repairing her energy field. She felt there were leakages in her system, and she had endured a long history of digestive problems. She also felt there were blocks to her full potential that needed to be removed.

As an experienced meditation teacher and hypnotherapist herself, Melissa relaxed easily to establish her expanded state of being.

As we expanded into her stored consciousness, Melissa was shown a very different version of herself than we would typically encounter. In this first stage of her journey, another self came through from an interdimensional existence. She was a few years older and carried contentment. She was poised and centered and had an air of clarity about her. Melissa noticed in this other her an absence of any confusion.

Melissa described her as being able to magnetize her energy from her core, and she had learned to do this from her heart center. She came from another universe where the energy is less heavy. When Melissa blended bodies with her, she could feel the difference and activated her heart center and crown. There was a tingling all through Melissa's body, and she moved around with jerky movements as all this took place. It was then that Melissa noted a significant difference between them: "There is a difference in our subatomic particles. Hers have not been distorted with confusion. Mine are contaminated with the culture here in our world."

This other version of our Melissa was able to share her experience of the other world she lived in, noting that it had two moons. She showed our Melissa a training facility where children were taught to move things with their minds. An intention of this perfect world was for the children to know their power so that they are not suppressed in any way. They worked to bring awareness to people about who they really are and taught this to their children.

The woman placed her hands on Melissa's forehead, telling her she "just had to remember." In her world, there was no question or doubt. Melissa felt as though her wings were spreading, her light expanding, and at the atomic level an explosion of light cascaded outward. In return, Melissa was able to offer her compassion, a reminder to her about what others are experiencing in her own world. This helped the woman understand that her knowing was truly an amazing thing. She then understood what it could be like if it wasn't there. This interaction was deep and powerful and was offered to Melissa as a resource for her journey, as we will soon understand.

As we expanded further into alternate consciousness, we met a younger version of Melissa who was around four years old, holding a doll that Melissa recognized from her childhood. This little girl was timid, gentle, and unsure, given the family circumstances of her life. She had come forward so Melissa could help her to be strong, and Melissa was able to bring the energy of deep love and acceptance she had been offered in the last realm to her younger self. The little girl's chest puffed out with this pride in being herself, and they both knew that from this time on, there would be "no more stumbling."

As always, we sent the ripple of healing through this realm and beyond. Something beautiful happened in this moment as Melissa was shown all the timelines that this would affect. Given the healing was felt so early in life as her four-year-old self, it was seen to occur before the creation of many other alternate realities. So many more of these realities benefited from future decisions that would be made, forming new realities from the healed energy now available to them. Melissa described them as "too many to count." She was shown a never-ending matrix of healing and felt the gratitude and peace they sent to her as a response to the healing ripple.

As we expanded into parallel consciousness, a group came forward to meet us. The 126 members of this group were many different lives currently being suppressed in other times and places on this earth. Again, using the energy gained from the first realm, Melissa sent a beam of light from her fingers to all of their foreheads. She sent them the Remembering of who they really are, and this moved from these parallel lives through all their own alternate realities. The healing was described as "astronomical."

Many of these lifetimes carried the energy of persecution as part of their suppression. Once this healing had taken place, they went back to their origins, which changed the structure of everything. Melissa described it like this: "They can redirect the energy flow of others around them, changing the outcomes of civilization—altering mankind in their times and places and the past of the earth. We are altering the consciousness of mankind at a very powerful level."

Our expansion continued into the interdimensional consciousness, where Melissa was met by a wise council of eight beings. They told Melissa they were a council of higher power and showed her the infinity symbol, saying that they existed in three dimensions of time. There were four on each side of her, and she was the intersection in the middle of the symbol. Melissa shared, "They have come to give awareness of where I've come from and to connect into my expansiveness. To show me the opposite of being small!"

Melissa felt herself as the link in the middle of the infinity symbol, knowing she was never alone. She explained, "If I visualize this, remember it, and bring it into me, it shows me expansiveness, collective consciousness, and the Remembering. The Remembering is key to knowing my magnificence and not being squashed into something I'm not. I sometimes go into the space of doubt."

We asked about the digestive issues, and Melissa reported, "It was a ball of fear, manifesting in the physical. It is exploded and gone—that was the leakage! We have placed the golden infinity symbol as a figure eight in the lower chakras. It is activating my universe within my body, and it will alter my cell membranes."

We then asked for change at the quantum level and were told we needed time for the physical body to integrate. As we moved into the eternal consciousness, Melissa summarized as follows: "I just have to believe and trust... one step at a time. The universe is coming to me with the opportunities to expand. I remain focused with intention, and power is bountiful now, not held back by the limiting energy structure. Simply focus intention on what you are looking for. There is a clearness of things manifesting—it is limitless now. Remember the expansiveness of who I am and what we can achieve when limitations and restrictions are gone. We have so much power; we just don't realize."

Melissa's case is a great example of how resources offered at the start of a journey can be used in every realm visited afterward. It indicates that these journeys we are observing, somehow tap into a higher order of things that go beyond the understanding of the client and even the facilitator. It really is an amazing universe when something shows up that will help before the issue is even presented, and we saw this in Melissa's first realm. Perhaps this is enabled by an intention that we as quantum consciousness facilitators hold in our belief, that our client has within their personal universe everything they will ever need to undertake healing or gather emerging wisdom. This is the facilitator's own creator effect, or given the entanglement with our clients, perhaps we should call it the creator "affect."

Melissa has experienced healing from all angles and has been working on her own self-development for years. Her feedback regarding the session neatly encapsulated the energy we observe during these experiences: "This is a delicate, refined, sweet, sensitive energy. There is no complexity of the trauma energy—no heaviness. It is energetically blissful!"

Case 15: Messages for Pete

There is one last case across the expanding realms of consciousness that I'd like to share, as it has also been instrumental to the work as it has evolved. This was one of my own early sessions, and I'd like to share it with you for a number of reasons. First, as an advocate for this work, it has been so important for me to see it from all angles, and I'm happy to share a story with you that is deep and personal to me as a client. Second, this case has strong and shaping messages from each of the realms that affect not just me but also send a rippling of knowing out, offered to the rest of us. Third, this case is a little different. While we have always "called forward" our other selves into a lighter healing, exploring energy, in this case I was actually taken to places and shown things. I was also very aware of additional guidance offered to me from one of my spiritual guides by the name of *Ra*. I felt his support and ultimately his cheeky sense of humor.

My facilitator was Melina, as she was so often in the early days of the work. She gently moved me out into the deeply expansive realms of my personal universe, holding my energy as only she can.

In my stored consciousness, my four-year-old self came forward and showed me a time when he was on a picnic rug at a park. Other family members had wandered off to use the public toilets close by, though in that moment he was left feeling alone and scared. I felt the need to step into the scene and pick him up and comfort him. As I felt into that little me, I knew his feelings, given the intanglement we feel with our other selves. Simply put, he wanted his mum. While this would be such a minor event in anyone's childhood, it was shown to me for a reason. It was about having a lack of dependence, and a powerful message flowed through to me: "In order to fully express your uniqueness, you can't be dependent on anyone else. You can connect and be synchronized and share and do all that, but each of us, in order to be the fully unique person that we are, has to shine in our own right, without dependence on anyone."

Ra then stepped in to support the message further. He talked about the fact that the books I write are just a start and to not be dependent on those either, as the work will evolve. Even books about this remarkable work are a snapshot in time. He told me "Little Pete" had a dependency on his mother in particular, which limited him. He told me that this is okay when we are young, but as we grow, we release that in order to shine to our full potential.

As we moved into my alternate consciousness, I was given one of the stronger messages I have ever received. I was taken to a funeral service and stood next to a coffin, looking down at myself. I had died at forty-seven years of age, and I saw my beautiful daughters and their mother in a deep state of distress. While it is rare in quantum consciousness work to have this type of experience, it was also one of the most freeing experiences of my life. Let me explain …

In this other reality, I had died on a train on my way to work in the corporate world. I was shown that I collapsed due to some form of a brain hemorrhage, followed by my heart giving out. I fell suddenly in an aisle of the train, and even though people tried to revive me, I was unresponsive. Ultimately, in the hospital some time later, my family had to make the difficult decision to turn off the life-support machine.

This other me was trapped in the system on a treadmill, believing that money—and all that it brings in terms of financial security and being a provider—was all that mattered. It is an illusion, as had I stayed in corporate life, I would not have been around to provide anyway.

The learnings of this realm were deep and shaping for me. I was shown the debilitating result of ignoring your purpose. I was also shown the flow-on impacts to others of my early exit and it was heartbreaking. The irony of that reality was not missed. I had made a life choice to be the best possible provider and had ended up providing nothing but sadness and devastation to the people I loved.

I was told to keep doing what I am doing and that everything is on track—in fact, it is unfolding "perfectly." Ra told me I had to undertake free will to build another reality, thereby creating a reality where I could build a model about the different realities. Then I could visit the other realities and learn from them so that I could share them in this reality. As he said this, he was laughing. The whole concept was just giving me a bit of a headache.

One clear message that came to me, though, was that here and now, this reality, is seen as "the ultimate reality." The reason is that in this reality we can access the learnings and wisdom and undertake healing from other realities as we need to.

Then, in turn, we can send those waves of greater consciousness rippling out holographically across all the others. You have to admit that is pretty cool.

Even though this realm had been so powerful, it was still just a part of the overall journey. As we entered the realm of parallel consciousness, I was met by two groups of people. On one side of me I saw all the lifetimes I am experiencing as a warrior, and on the other all the lifetimes I am experiencing as a healer. I recognized some of these people from other sessions I'd undertaken over the years. The dynamic between the two groups was fascinating. The warriors never liked the healers and the healers never really liked the warriors. I stood between the two groups as a bridge, as I carried the characteristics of both groups. They looked at me in disbelief and asked, "How can that be so? It is like being a man and a woman at the same time." I sense this may have been more the warriors talking at this time ...

I stood before all of them and talked about what they could really be and who they really are. I spoke to them about being warriors for the light and healers of the light, a chance to stand firm for deep and powerful healing and to come together and bridge their two worlds that have had such different histories through the ages. I was able to bring them closer under this united purpose and saw them shaking hands, ready to learn from each other.

I was offered the following message:

Often Pete chooses warrior first and healer second, when it should be healer first and warrior second. It is about reversing the order in which he moves through those situations as they arise.

The old shamans are seen as warriors when they simply stand their ground.

Be a warrior from integrity and not from anger. Stand in the integrity and share the power of what you stand for. People won't stand behind you when you respond from anger unless it pulls on their own anger and indignation. If you make a stand on principle and integrity, people will come with you.

I was told this message was very important, and as I received it, the last of my old corporate leadership energy drifted quietly into the background...and then the journey through my personal universe continued.

As we expanded out into my interdimensional consciousness, I felt myself flashing past planets and felt I was being shown the size of the universe as well as something that was far away from me, both in distance and culture. I was shown two different types of life-forms.

The first was a race of beings who had built an artificial vehicle to hold consciousness. This thing they constructed looked a bit like a household appliance, and I have affectionately referred to this from that time onward as "my life as a toaster."

The intention of this race was to preserve consciousness so that it wouldn't be lost. The error in their approach was that they didn't realize that consciousness continued beyond physical existence and in fact by trying to contain it, they were holding it back. The lessons here were simple: consciousness cannot be contained, and it can take many different forms.

Ra chimed in with a message at this time, becoming serious for a change: "In terms of the places you can go to, see, or experience, they are limitless. Absolutely limitless. What is helpful in this case is to expand your horizons. Pete is still carrying some of his human beliefs, which is why he is having problems understanding their culture."

And I was. This was quite foreign to me as I tried later on to integrate the experience into my human existence. This resulted in a change to the guidance we offer as quantum consciousness facilitators as clients move into the realm of interdimensional consciousness.

I was then shown a second type of life form, a sphere with blue energy all around it, a different dimensional consciousness. Again, I was offered some deeper insights into myself:

This is a place where the intellect is honed and offers a sense of why he has at times been emotionally reluctant. He learned in this mental world to pull into the intellect, to understand what is going on in tough energy … just like he observes automatically sometimes, from the experience of this lifetime.

We are like a piece of consciousness. There is an interchange between this central blue sphere and us that just hones our understanding of things. It is almost a telepathic learning process, like a school. It helps us understand the energy of emotions so as not to get caught up in them.

This was helpful in allowing me to understand the vastly different experiences in consciousness and how even something as different as this life around the blue sphere could have a ripple effect back into how I pull back to observe emotions from time to time ... in balance with being an empath!

As we expanded finally into the eternal consciousness, I spent time just enjoying the complete absence of any physical restrictions. As I joined with the fabric of the cosmos, I seemed so far away from everything. The things that had seemed so important as I traversed the realms of my personal universe just fell away ... For the first time, I was able to experience what it felt like to be part of all there is.

I was able to start the journey back to the forever-changed present consciousness, bringing the planets, the stars, and the universe with me ...

As Melina gently guided me backward through the realms, I was able to articulate the learnings I had been offered:

I knew firsthand that I was part of the fabric of the cosmos in a way that I didn't before. I had my own validation of what we all want to believe from what we have been told. I felt connected to everything, in a way I had never been before.

I understood that consciousness is not in the body, it cannot be contained, and when freed, it moves more naturally into its most powerful state. This was seen as an important message to share with others through writings and workshops, anytime and anyplace.

My leadership would change so that I would become more of the healer than the warrior. I could change this to bring more of the energy of "the statesman," a term I was offered as a way to anchor and capture the energy of that leadership style.

I glowed with the knowledge that pursuing my purpose was the best way to look after the people I love. The alternative was literally a dead end. That day, two worlds blended together in an energy of passionate freedom to be me. I could only offer my authentic self; there actually was no other choice.

I finally understood that in order to shine fully, you can't be dependent on anything or anyone. When you break the dependency, then you can shine in ways that you could not have otherwise. We have greater potential than we could ever know, and the release of any conditioning we hold puts it within our grasp.

I returned to my forever-changed present consciousness. As with these experiences, I was reflective and a little disoriented as I allowed the learnings to seep into this time and place. The conversation with Melina was invaluable. She continued to hold sacred space, while together we joined some of the dots.

We learned firsthand that the importance of the role of the quantum consciousness facilitator is to have a conversation following the session that honors the client and reminds them that access to their personal universe will be with them forevermore.

As I continued to absorb the wisdom offered from my journey, I started to see a theme emerging about balance. Our world is out of balance, and the best way to contribute to the rebalancing of a troubled world is through our own personal universe.

We have to find the balance between dependency and potential, between this reality and alternate realities we have formed. I need to balance the warrior and the healer to embrace the statesman. We must achieve balance between freeing our consciousness completely and being in a body to undertake our purpose. Once we can rebalance ourselves, we can offer to the world our own ripple effect that will serve our planet, humanity … and beyond, through our own personal universe and out into the fabric of the cosmos.

A Comment on the Quantum Consciousness Experience

As mentioned earlier in this book, this work is still in its early days. At this stage of our research in 2018, we have over five hundred cases behind our Institute for Quantum Consciousness, though this number is growing as we receive and process further cases from our network of facilitators and they take the work forward in their own practices.

This work is deep and profound at best and surprising and even contemplative at the very least. We have seen that people who have experience in expanded states of awareness, who can "let go" and trust what comes, seem to have the most significant experiences. It is the ability and preparedness to transcend the human aspects of ourselves that offers the most remarkable journeys.

Even by reading this book, you have signaled to the universe that you are ready to understand that there is so much more to you than meets the eye. The Remembering of this is all you need to bring new insight, hope, and inspiration to yourself and those around you.

I'd like to pause and recognize those who have offered their personal experiences for this book so we could tell their stories to make a difference in the lives of others. We send ripples of gratitude to those people so they can understand more deeply their sacred contribution to the evolution of consciousness on this planet.

11

CHANGING THE LANDSCAPE OF PLANET EARTH

We have been blessed with a remarkable planet. This sentient being on which we make our home is a finely tuned ecosystem, rich in diversity of landscape, plant life, and animal life. We don't have to look far to observe the wonders all around us, whether they be deserted beaches, forests of ancient redwoods, or mountain peaks that reach to the sky. Nature is blessed with shape and color that, when looked at closely, show the secrets of creation and the key to a safe and natural environment.

You see, nature is perfect and always has been. The lesson we sometimes miss is that humanity is also perfect, simply because we are part of nature. This is so often forgotten. We have within us incredible potential that remains untapped. We have physical and energetic healing systems that we don't fully understand and an eternal consciousness residing within us. We possess the innate ability to tap into a quantum world through intention, so what we may have once perceived as paranormal becomes normal, and the supernatural becomes natural.

Our deeper beliefs hold us in the status quo.

My experience of working with organizational cultures is that the "home culture" prevails, unless a dedicated shift is resourced substantially and is effectively implemented. I remember a conversation with the leader of an organization. He had recruited a couple of new subordinates with the expectation of a resultant overnight change—which subsequently failed. We had an enlightening conversation regarding how people assimilate into new workplace teams, merging into the collective consciousness of the current workplace culture. It is my experience of group culture that though they may well have espoused values, philosophies, and rules, it is the leaders' behavior as role models that truly define the prevailing culture. These people mold the energy of the group, and their personal and then collective intentions, beliefs, and values truly define the journey of the organization.

At the personal level, we are the same. The prevailing culture of the collective community of our various selves sometimes needs work to release the limitations that we hold. For over a decade, I've worked with anxiety and depression in clinical practice, and it was only when I came to know these conditions as energetic blockages, and not a form of mental illness, that I was able to assist people to shift the energy and step into their true potential. Tracing this energy to the beliefs that hold us in place can't be done entirely with cognitive behavioral therapy processes. Simply put, much of these restrictions are held subconsciously and even energetically. The energetic distress can stem from unresolved childhood issues in the formative years or even before birth or from energy passed on through family culture from previous generations. Other sources include unaddressed grief and bereavement, past traumatic events, and even energetic intrusions held in the energy field.

Ultimately, the underlying belief in these types of conditions comes down to a single principle: "Am I safe?" This question is the underpinning survival program of all species and has been so since they came into being. This is programming at the most basic level and also forms the foundational level of all consciousness and evolutionary models. You simply can't evolve if you aren't safe, as your attention is drawn to the survival basics like food, water, and shelter both for yourself and those you care for.

Or so it would seem.

There is only one true catalyst for change, and I've mentioned this to hundreds of people over the years either in groups or as individuals: the only true catalyst for change is dissatisfaction with the current state. Humanity is in the unique position where we can actually evolve, merely through our intention to do so. In Abraham Maslow's hierarchy of needs, this principle is referred to as "self-actualization." This is where a person's desire for self-fulfillment leads to the achievement of their potential. Richard Barrett's Seven Levels of Consciousness Model assimilates and extends Maslow's and describes the fourth level (transformation), where we move from the levels of self-interest toward the levels of common good.[32] David Hawkins's map of

---

32. Richard Barrett, "The Barrett Model," Barrett Values Centre, accessed February 12, 2018, https://www.valuescentre.com/mapping-values/barrett-model.

consciousness measures the calibration of events, objects, and even people through the muscle testing of applied kinesiology. When the measurement of 200 ("courage") or even beyond is obtained, there is a positive contribution to the overall calibration of humanity.[33] Don Beck and Chris Cowan's concept of Spiral Dynamics, initiated by Clare Graves in the 1960s, talks about humanity reaching a second-tier evolution as some of the former paradigms of management and leadership fall away, giving way to a new way of being.

So, in summary, we have an incredible opportunity to take humanity to the next level, but do we have enough dissatisfaction with the current state to mobilize our collective consciousness to do so? What are the beliefs that keep us bound in this state, and how can we transcend these to move into a new paradigm of existence?

If we could release the needs and subsequent fears that keep us at the lower levels of all consciousness models and move upward ...

If we could embrace the potential of the quantum realm that carries so many messages of our innate potential waiting to be activated ...

If we could experience the expanded states of awareness, releasing us from the restrictions of this physical realm and explore the universe itself ...

Humanity will evolve in ways we simply can't imagine.

---

33. David Hawkins, *Power vs. Force: The Hidden Determinants of Human Behavior* (Carlsbad, CA: Hay House, 1995), 105–106.

Humanity's Prevailing Mindsets

There are a number of mindsets that are continually reinforced by our existing culture, our heritage, and the systems in which we exist. They have evolved into their current vibration through a number of factors, such as wealth creation for financial success, business competition, and increased pace of lifestyle. These systems interweave with self-supporting structures.

The majority of my own experiences in these systems has been in the Western world, Australia in particular, so the comments and examples certainly carry that flavor. The critical imperative is that, in the longer term, these mindsets are not in the interest of our evolution as a species to a higher way of being. They are flawed and form part of our conditioning, permeating our subconscious, as part of a prevailing global culture.

The purpose of this chapter is not to extend conspiracy theories or move into the energy of accusations or anger with the current state of humanity's consciousness. All we need to understand is that the prevailing mindsets hold us back from being the best we can be. These mindsets are permeated with the energy of fear and survival, simply because we have forgotten that we have the potential to control our own destiny. I also offer that all over the world, there are great stories of those who continue to break the existing paradigms of their day.

History records such people as Galileo and Copernicus, who theorized that the earth was not the center of the universe. Ferdinand Magellan refused to believe he would sail off the edge of the world. Nikola Tesla invented a device for free energy. His ideas still come up from time to time in conversation as we continue to seek solutions to rapidly diminishing fossil fuels.

For those who wish to delve further into research behind the mindsets and agendas linked to them, there is an abundance of information available on the internet. A good start point is Foster and Kimberly Gamble's Thrive movement, and people can determine their own viewpoint from the evidence provided.

Mindset 1: "I must create financial wealth to survive, and the more I have the happier I'll be."

There is a fundamental flaw in the logic that leads to the life-long goal of the creation of financial wealth. We spend a lifetime meeting financial obligations and achieving wealth goals just so we can pass over in our final moments and leave it all behind. Ultimately, contrary to what the ancient Egyptians believed when they buried their pharaohs with accumulated wealth, food for the journey, and their entourage of slaves ... we simply can't take it with us.

In Australia in the 1950s, we were blessed with a migration scheme that offered a new energy of multiculturalism and gave opportunities to people coming from an ever-repairing war-torn Europe. As a result, "between 1945 and 1965 more than two million migrants came to Australia." [34] They came to be part of the "Lucky Country," and boom times of economic growth allowed for good prospects of employment and the chance to own your own home in a safe country, where you could raise a family.

34. "1945–1965: New Australia," *Objects through Time* exhibition, Migration Heritage Centre, Accessed March 8, 2018, http://www.migrationheritage.nsw.gov.au/exhibition/objectsthroughtime-history/1945-1965/index.html.

Owning one's own home became possible for anybody willing to work hard. The basic needs of food, water, and shelter were more easily achieved, and people established a lifestyle in which they could enjoy their time on the planet and think about how they would help their children achieve the same.

The energy of abundance was established, though something else started to emerge as well. There was something in the assumption that "if I have an even greater abundance, I will become even happier." The need to have "abundant survival" became the need to have greater wealth, and the age of consumerism and wealth creation started to form in the decades following.

In my hometown of Melbourne, Australia, the average price of a home in 1973 was A$19,800. In 2014, this rose to A$615,068, which is thirty-one times higher. In the same period, the average weekly wage increased also from A$111.80 to A$1,453.90. In comparison, this is only thirteen times higher.[35] For many, the dream to own their homes has slipped away, unless they change their focus from lifestyle to financial earnings.

I remember learning basic commerce as a subject in school and spending some class time on differentiating a "need" from a "want." It was clear back then which was which, though now we have been influenced to remove that line. Much of this has to do with how advertising has permeated our media. This advertising is subliminal, and as someone who has spent a great

---

35. BT, "Australian House Prices: Then and Now [Domain, 2014]," *Living in Tanareit* (blog), March 25, 2017, adaptation of Nicole Thomas, "Australian House Prices: Then and Now," on Domain.com (page discontinued), https://livingintarneit.wordpress.com/2015/03/25/australian-house -prices-then-and-now-domain-2014/.

deal of time working in people's subconscious minds, I would have to say that it is very effective. Simply put, we now believe our wants are actually our needs.

The new car, the bigger house, the better job, and the yearning for more material possessions are now part of the journey that we undertake under our own free will, with the subconscious influence of the drive toward materialism we see in Western culture. This is a cycle that continues under the flow-on belief that when the happiness of a new possession fades, we seek the next one on our pilgrimage toward that illusive happiness. Then the next possession and the next... always seeking and never finding, simply because we are looking in the wrong place.

This culture draws on two things. First, we have an underlying program as human beings to stay safe and to survive. If we are offered an opportunity to move further away from financial insecurity, we will take it. Even though we may transcend the need for survival, we continue to satisfy this already-met need from the conditioning of our society. Second, we have a deeper yearning to self-actualize, to realize we are more than we believe ourselves to be, and to search further for some form of evolution. It is the nature of all consciousness to evolve, though mostly we try to meet this need while being in an unaware state.

So the spiral continues. To get the bigger house, you need the better job, which pays the better salary, which allows for a bigger mortgage, which gets the bigger house... and so on. The better salary means higher contributions toward retirement and thus greater feelings of safety as you near retirement age. Later on, this also offers more resources to ultimately enter the aged care system. That system is expensive and drains the resources built up over your lifetime. Those who inherit your accumulated wealth then have a smaller portion and need to stay in the system as well to meet their own "needs," which are really "wants." It is a confusing cycle, though particularly well embedded.

This cycle is also helpful to the government for the different taxes we pay. Higher salary means more income tax, and more disposable income leads to higher consumerism, which means more consumption tax. Moving to a bigger and better property means more land tax and stamp duty on the sale. Ultimately, a larger mortgage means bigger mortgage payments, banking fees, and interest paid. We work hard all our lives to satisfy and propagate the cycle, to become part of a system that some decades ago offered security and loving nurture for ourselves and loved ones. Somewhere along the way the rules seem to have changed without our noticing.

At the organizational level, this plays out as well. The goals of most organizations are financial, and they watch their markets, their competitors, and their bottom line. Often, they are accountable to shareholders or, at the very least, business owners. Ultimately, some organizations embrace what they call the "triple bottom line," which measures financial, social, and environmental value, and do many good works or have sustainability and environmentally friendly initiatives.[36] These are creating a higher consciousness, as long as they aren't intended as a way to offer differentiation from other share purchases, underpinned

---

36. "Triple Bottom Line (TBL)," Investopedia, accessed April 24, 2017, https://www.investopedia.com/terms/t/triple-bottom-line.asp.

by that same consciousness of wealth at the organizational level, otherwise known as profitability.

In this moment, people around the world are trying to get through pop-up ads on their computer or their mobile phone just to get to the information they need. Someone is sitting in their lounge room, watching cable television and remembering why they first purchased it—as it once had no commercials. Someone else is clearing the spam advertising in their email inbox. Someone is receiving a sales call from someone they never heard of, and, finally, a wealthy person is wondering why they still aren't happy. These behaviors we see simply indicate the prevailing and limiting mindset of financial wealth creation as the path to happiness.

Let's move past this stereotyping for a moment. The fact that you are reading this book indicates you are in the process of breaking the paradigm of this mindset or have already done so. For you, "dissatisfaction with the current state" may have already occurred. Let's pause to acknowledge you and others who are already breaking the traditional mindsets and bringing a new energy to the existence of planet earth. Just know that every conversation we have about building consciousness takes humanity closer to the transcendence of reality as we know it and offers something greater for us to aspire to. We simply have to release the things that hold us back.

Mindset 2: "The medical system maintains my well-being."

The move toward materialism and profitability has also permeated our medical systems. While medical science has made some tremendous breakthroughs in recent years, access to these new miracles comes at a price.

It is remarkable that an organ can be transplanted from one human being to another. However, the cost of this procedure is estimated to be around A$139,900 for a heart transplant and A$134,600 for a lung transplant in New South Wales.[37] Medications too are on the rapid increase in terms of usage.

In January 2012, the *Sydney Morning Herald* reported on a survey funded by the Australian federal government that showed that "nearly half of people aged 50 or older take at least five drugs or supplements on a typical day." Further, "Cholesterol-lowering treatment use has increased six-fold since 1995 ... and the proportion of people taking an antidepressant has nearly trebled."[38] There has been a marked increase in the use of antidepressants and antipsychotics even in adolescents. In June 2014, a news article released by the Australian Broadcasting Commission stated that between 2009 and 2012, "the number of children aged between 10 and 14 given antidepressants jumped by more than a third, while anti-psychotic medications rose by almost 50 per cent."[39] Painkiller medications

37. "Cost of Care in NSW Hospitals," NSW Government, last modified March 23, 2016, http://www.health.nsw.gov.au/Hospitals/Going_To_hospital /cost-of-care/Pages/default.aspx.

38. Julie Robotham, "Huge Increase in the Use of Prescription Drugs in Those over 50," *Sydney Morning Herald*, January 16, 2012, http://www .smh.com.au/national/health/huge-increase-in-the-use-of-prescription -drugs-among-those-over-50-20120115-1q1fj.html#ixzz3B6MiMfJy.

39. Sophie Scott, "Anti-depressant, Anti-psychotic Medication Prescriptions for Kids on the Rise, Study Finds," ABC News, last modified June 18, 2014, http://www.abc.net.au/news/2014-06-19/anti-depressant- prescriptions-for-kids-on-the-rise-study-says/5534530.

are also on the increase. Prescriptions for oxycodone (a morphine-based painkiller typically prescribed for acute, chronic, and cancer-related pain) increased by 152 percent between 2002 and 2003 and between 2007 and 2008. Another study showed a 180 percent increase between 2002 and 2009.[40]

The organizations that manufacture prescription drugs are, by their very nature, moving to meet financial goals. The Australian Pharmaceutical Benefits Scheme enables discounts on certain medications, though it perpetuates the current mindsets by subsidizing consumer dependence on the medications concerned.

I have many conversations with clients who wish to remove their dependence on prescription medications. They are tired of feeling "emotionally leveled out," and while the anxiety is minimized, so is the joy. Many describe to me that they feel they aren't fully in life. They state their intention to be ready to address the underlying issues that are the true source of the energy trapped within them.

I acknowledge and thank these courageous souls who come to see me. For them, dissatisfaction with their own emotive state has driven them onward to find new solutions, embracing alternative health practices as a way to take control of their lives once again.

Mindset 3: "The authorities have my best interests at heart."

The role of the government is difficult in a changing world. In the Western world, officials are entrusted by the people

---

40. Gina McKeon, "Oxycodone: The Factors behind Australians' Increasing Use of 'Hillbilly Heroin,'" ABC News, last modified April 29, 2014, http://www.abc.net.au/news/2014-04-07/oxycodone-use-on-the-rise-in -australia/5372146.

through an election process to meet our needs and keep us safe. Indeed, this need for safety and financial health permeates Western culture as well.

Governments mainly measure their success by financial means, whether it be through the health of the economy, the gross domestic product, the general cost of living, inflation rates, or public spending across portfolios such as health and education. This brings only a limited perspective.

A trend in recent times in Australia, due mainly to an aging population, is to remove the old paradigm of the government providing a retirement allowance—a pension. This old thought pattern of the past generations was that we pay taxes all our lives, and then when we retire, we receive a pension in gratitude for a lifetime of service. This paradigm has been broken now with the advent of superannuation (retirement) schemes, with a gradually increasing percentage of people's salaries being set aside for the future. The taxes are still in place, and these have been modified and extended over the years, with new ones being introduced. An example of this is the goods and services tax, a consumption tax introduced into Australia in the year 2000. A system has emerged in which we are taxed on our earned incomes, pay tax whenever we make purchases, now save for our own retirement, and, if we manage to have any savings of our own put aside, we are taxed on the interest earned.

The democratic system of government is based on holding an election so that the people can decide who leads a nation. This imperative has great intentions, though it also is an energetic drain on both the elected and opposition parties. Much of the final year of an election period is spent campaigning for reelection. That process of aggressive and often defamatory energy drains the viability and often credibility of both parties and takes them away from the core imperative of what they were elected to do—govern on behalf of the people and make our world a better place.

However, there are some people who want to make a difference, and they start new political parties or enter politics with high ideals. History is full of people who rebelled against the current system and challenged the leaders of the day or forced change through their own spirited determination and revolutionary ideas. We must acknowledge and support the free thinkers who challenge the status quo and show courage in the face of adversity. They do so with a gentle power and intention, and rather than drive their own agenda from anger or fear, they bring forward a revolutionary mindset. These are the people who will change the world, and we must encourage them to come to power in a way that allows the creation of a new paradigm.

In 1989, the world was shocked by the events in China and the student massacre in Tiananmen Square, when those who wanted a different world were crushed by those who held the power of authority. The following day as the tanks rolled down Chang'an Avenue, a man carrying a couple of shopping bags stepped in front of the column of advancing armor. He came to be known as the "Tank Man." Unable to move around him as he continually repositioned to block their path, the entire column of tanks stopped.

Small acts of courage against the status quo of the day can start a change to our world.

The Interweave of the Current Systems

The prevailing mindsets are quite clear. What appears to be a progressive and modern society carries an underlying energy that draws on the human programming of needing to be safe. This basic human need for survival that we are dealing with comes from the core of our being and the basic wiring of us as a survival species. We entrust our livelihoods to a system that is based on a survival consciousness that has been extended into consumerism. The current system is so permeated with this culture that it may not be able to be repaired; in fact, it most likely needs to be replaced. The current system is firmly embedded in government and our medical industry and has moved though large-scale organizations into our food and water systems as well as our utilities and services, cascading down to small business and even us as consumers.

However, there is a ray of hope beneath all this. We can establish a new way of being, a blending of new mindsets that allows for the introduction of a new way of thinking, a new energy and collective intention for humanity.

The first of these new mindsets is to embrace the new science and know at the core of our being that we are quantum beings in a quantum universe, full of potential yet to be discovered. We are energy, consciousness, and the creators of own destiny. We must be the change we want to see in the world, as we are all masters of our personal universe. Once we let go of the prevailing mindsets we have been offered, we literally become a world of possibilities.

The second of these new mindsets embraces an ever-growing phenomenon much ignored by medical science and psychological models. Our consciousness does not need a body to exist, and if we were to know this with absolute certainty from our own experience, just imagine what that would do to our need for human safety! The greatest fear of all, the fear of death that underpins all others, would then become irrelevant. The survival instincts of our species are part of our human wiring, not part of our expanded states.

If we put the two of these together, we become an expanded consciousness embracing the quantum realm.

We become quantum consciousness, and if we could all hold that knowing, then it would simply be a case of living in that forever-connected human consciousness, in a way that transcends the prevailing mindsets of our society.

As the collective consciousness of humanity, this would ripple from us as individuals through families and communities, and then nations, and, finally, the globe into a different way of being.

12

THE EVOLVED LANDSCAPE
OF PLANET EARTH

We are told by quantum theorists of the endless possibilities for us available in the Many Worlds theory. In the book *The Fabric of the Cosmos*, quantum physicist Brian Greene tells us that "the concept of 'the universe' is enlarged to include innumerable 'parallel universes' ... so that anything quantum mechanics predicts *could* happen ... does happen." [41]

So let us envision, or even bring into being through our intention, a different earth that exists under a different set of prevailing mindsets:

1. We are all connected, and that which affects one affects all.

2. Our reason for being is to raise our own and others' vibrations.

---

41. Greene, *The Fabric of the Cosmos,* 205.

3. We are the custodians of the earth, and her well-being is our legacy to future generations.

Evolved Mindsets for Humanity

A planet embracing these mindsets may have the following characteristics:

Mindset 1: "We are all connected, and that which affects one affects all."

This world carries a majority population in a global middle class. There are still geographical pockets of the world where the absence of resources and the impacts of natural disasters bring a greater need, though as they emerge over time, there is an immediate and global response.

The geographical boundaries between countries are therefore more relaxed, and citizenship is embraced at a global level. Clearly identified cultures bring a local diversity that draws on the history of local places.

The whole world understands that the global chain of collective consciousness is only as strong as the weakest link, so that is where resources are applied as required. The economic class structure has dissolved in most of the geographies, morphing more into the global middle class mentioned, with access to food, water, technology, and educational opportunities. All these are managed on a regional basis.

The overall health of this global society is measured and compared by regions of the world. The benchmarks established cover quality of education, spiritual growth, sustainability, and of course the quality of basic needs such as food, water, and shelter. There is also a fulfilment index that draws on regional happiness and joy in regard to life itself. This is done with the sole intention of highlighting best-practice regions so they can assist others in achieving the same standard through the donation and sharing of know-how, skills, and expertise.

The regions are led by teams of philanthropists, who work globally from local knowledge, bridging the smaller community and larger regional models. These leaders are democratically elected by their regional areas, on the basis of personal ethics, visionary practices, and experience in leading people from a selfless viewpoint across numerous roles of ever-increasing responsibility.

At the individual level, people have access to the resources that meet all their needs. They are up to date with technology and connected to other people globally through that technology. Leaders in small communities are responsible for the communication in both directions, and at all levels there is a culture of openness and honesty, as information is shared readily and easily.

Mindset 2: "Our reason for being is to raise our own and others' vibrations."

A number of consciousness models are used at the different levels of society, from the global down through regional and then to local measurement. Annually, the consciousness of individuals is measured by the teams in local communities, and all progress, regardless how large or small, is celebrated, though there is greater fulfilment when groups contribute as a collective to overall consciousness. Each year the amalgamated results show the progress of humanity globally.

People enthusiastically share ideas for growth and evolution at both the individual and group levels, knowing of the contribution to the collective. Individuals who find this type of focus more difficult are allocated a consciousness mentor, usually selected from a group of local elders.

All trade, service, and product initiatives contribute to a "consciousness commerce." Currency is of a vibrational nature, and generous barter and fair exchange are the hallmarks of trade at the local and even global level.

The local roles and even career paths are focused toward contribution beyond self. When the possibility is offered to receive, it is accepted with grace and appreciation, knowing that this act is in itself a contribution to another, providing a chance to offer them the experience of gifting their services.

Mindset 3: "We are the custodians of the earth, and her well-being is our legacy to future generations."
It was deemed that the use of fossil fuels would be detrimental to the planet, and thus a range of natural energy resources were developed. Depending on the part of the world you live in, access to solar or wind power is the preferred approach. A range of smaller sustainable energy resources are also used, from tidal power to gas power recycled from specially treated organic waste.

Most fruit and vegetables are grown locally based on the regional conditions and are consumed close to their harvest time and place, each region being self-sufficient for both their production and consumption. When an oversupply occurs, trade and donation with other regional areas takes place.

Housing is environmentally friendly and harmonious with surrounding local landscapes. The local communities have best-practice guidelines on infrastructure and size of the community in relation to resources close at hand. Different community models are offered depending on community size, resources at hand, and climatic conditions. New communities are set up in periods of stronger growth, and the more experienced communities mentor the leaders of new and emerging ones.

Every community at all levels has sustainability and recycling programs, while education systems firmly embrace the concept of global legacy to their next generation of descendants.

Summary

The description above is designed to set an aspiration for how we can be. It would be wonderful to live in a world where the Western medical and the long-standing alternative-health industries worked hand in hand with the client or patient at the center of their focus. It would be amazing to find global financial systems that target a distribution of wealth that meets everybody's needs—a world without poverty, starvation, or unaddressed disease. It would be inspirational if the core focus of industry, at all levels, was sustainability of our natural environment first and foremost and profitability second. Ultimately, our future as a species will be driven by the prevailing mindsets of humanity, though there is hope, as we know that a small group of people can at times change the world.

In his book *The Divine Matrix*, author Gregg Braden summarizes the impact of prevailing mindsets well in his comment that "we can't change a reality if we remain in the same consciousness that made it."[42] Our first step is to change our thinking, and the second step is to ripple this out holographically through the collective consciousness of humanity. So how can this actually be done?

Thoughts are starting to shift in small pockets of humanity. The consciousness community is growing daily, much of it leveraging and building on the new science that is quantum physics and the possibilities contained for humanity. So many new horizons, so many amazing opportunities for planet earth, as our mindsets start to change, and we ripple that out through others. Braden describes this ripple of consciousness as the "'Maharishi Effect' in honor of Maharishi Mahesh Yogi, who stated that when one percent of a population practiced the methods of meditation that he offered, there would be a reduction in violence and crime for that population."[43]

A number of studies have documented what has come to be known as the *super radiance effect*. Ultimately, it was found that merely a small number of people was required to become a catalyst: Braden notes in the sixteenth key in his twenty keys of conscious creation that "the minimum number of people required to 'kick-start' a change in consciousness is the $\sqrt{1\%}$ of a

42. Braden, *Divine Matrix*, 81.

43. Braden, *Divine Matrix*, 115.

population."[44] If we take 1 percent of the seven billion people we have in the world, we end up with a figure of seventy million. The square root of this number is approximately 8,367 people. I wonder how many are already out there kick-starting this shift in consciousness.

One of the ways we retain the existing prevailing mindsets is in our subconscious. While we can have every conscious creative intention in the beta brain wave patterns of the conscious mind, it's the larger impact of this so often unacknowledged repository of energy, held deeper within ourselves, that can scuttle the very best of intentions.

In my last book, *Hypnoenergetics—The Four Dimensions*, I talk about the conscious mind being the piece above the water in the old iceberg analogy. Indeed, we are so often held back by those deeply embedded beliefs that lie in the larger 90 percent under the surface. I want to stress also that, as a longtime hypnotherapist and energy practitioner, I've discovered that the subconscious is not part of our brain. It's actually the energy of our energy field, more easily accessed through expanded states. However, I do regard the conscious mind as being more of a thinking and integration tool.

Simply put, when we are in the conscious state, we are in our thinking and analysis form, which is reflected in brainwave patterns of the beta range (roughly 12 to 30 cycles per second). When we move below that level into the subconscious, superconscious (as per Michael Newton's research), and even collective consciousness (or collective unconscious, as per Carl Jung et al.), we open a whole new territory. The language of

---

44. Braden, *Divine Matrix*, 208–209.

the waking conscious mind is *time*, the language of the subconscious and deeper is *energy* held in wide and various forms as we tap into what Braden calls the Divine Matrix.

In chapter 2, there is more on both why consciousness is not held in the brain and on the matrix described by Braden, within the information on various leaders in the consciousness community. Those mentioned in that chapter, and others like them, are the people driving the paradigms that will evolve global consciousness.

CONCLUSION:
AN EVOLVED CONSCIOUSNESS
FOR HUMANITY

So where to from here?

This book is offered to you as an opportunity for hope and inspiration, in a world that has too many shadows and not enough light. The question that remains now is, how do you want to seek and build your light? The beauty of all this is that it already resides within you, powerful and unique, a perceived single shard of light that connects you intimately to a wave of light that encompasses all there is.

Let's return momentarily to quantum physics and that "paradigm buster," the now-famous double-slit experiment that we talked about at the start of this book. Is it a particle or is it a wave? Are you a particle or are you a wave?

This startling discovery at the subatomic level is the validation you seek. You are a particle *and* a wave. You are made up of the same matter as galaxies; you are a universe, an immortal being, and a portal to all you have ever been, can now become, and eternally will be. You are your own unique being *and* you are the fabric of the cosmos. Welcome to this Remembering of who you really are …

Now what will you do with this information? Will you choose to stay small, or will you reach into the cosmos to understand more deeply your own divinity?

I do not advocate that you do anything in particular. I only suggest that you do something or become different as a result of this knowing.

If I were asked to suggest ways forward, then I would offer you five things.

1. Explore

Seek, as this starts the journey.

The major way we find information now is via the internet. There are an unlimited number of blogs and websites, and my experience is that many of them carry opinions, beliefs, and sometimes even well-disguised doctrine. We are bombarded by advertising designed to encourage us to purchase products and services so we can remain part of the materialism model. This is why I mainly recommend books, as I feel they hold a purer energy.

Authors answer a call to offer others their own unique wisdom. Let's remember that books have always been the vehicle through which wisdom has been passed on through generations. If we unplugged the internet and technology were no longer available, web-based information would disappear. To be honest, I'd be okay with that and would then sit comfortably in front of my own bookshelf, flicking through already dog-eared pages of amazing books, absorbing the wisdom, till I'm called to leave this body and become part of the greater universe I already know myself to be.

Another deep aspect of exploration can be to go within and find your hidden authenticity, thus becoming free. This is not about going to a psychic and hearing someone tell you your story. This is about finding the deep and personal inspiration that comes from remembering who you already are.

The journey toward this may involve healing initially, as you peel away layers of energies that have affected your life without you even being aware. Find the right person to help you, and I encourage so very strongly, that you check the credentials of the people you work with. Find a person who embraces a greater purpose beyond themselves as they offer you their professional services. That energy comes from the purpose of their soul and transcends human influences.

As a longtime practitioner, teacher, and leader in the alternate health industry internationally, I wish to offer to you that many are not what they seem. Our industry too has its charlatans and opportunists. I suggest you don't believe all that you read on people's websites. Look for credentials that offer outside validation of their skills. Look for memberships of professional associations that have high standards of entry, which can only be achieved by comprehensive training. I offer the example that there are thousands of trained hypnotherapists in Australia, though a far smaller number number join hypnotherapy associations that are members of the self-regulating industry body, the Hypnotherapy Council of Australia.

Feel free to ask people how extensive their training has been, whether they carry professional insurance, and what code of ethics they are bound by. These points are so important, as they help you identify the hobbyist versus the professional in practice. Please bear in mind too that all good practitioners usually grow from a hobbyist into a professional as their purpose emerges.

Feel the energy of the person, first through their website or their conversation. Use your intuition, as it will serve you well. It is, after all, connected to your soul.

The best possible way to find the right person is the same as it has been down through the ages. It is simply word of mouth from someone that you trust.

In the resources section at the end of the book, I will offer some further information.

2. Be Courageous

Actually, you already are, given you chose to incarnate here.

At a deeper level, you have purpose either unfolding already or waiting to be remembered. Listen to your soul and hear the voice within that will guide you toward your ultimate state of being. Feel into the synchronicities and learn to follow your intuition. The path of least resistance will emerge as the right way to go, once you release anything that is in the way.

Take the small steps: sign up for a course you may feel drawn toward, join a meditation circle, try past-life regression with a credible hypnotherapist, or have a kinesiology session. Perhaps buy a book on spirituality, energy, or quantum physics for the general public.

There may be people who will think less of you as you no longer fit their paradigm, though I'd simply offer to you that that's okay. Remember that any dependency on the good opinion of others will only dampen your light. You simply need to find new people, those who build your energy and with whom you can have the deeper conversations that you seek. Ask for them to come to you, and the universe will respond.

Push the boundaries of your own emergence and you will evolve, despite internal or external resistance as you are moving toward your more natural state.

3. Understand Your Ripple Effect

Whatever you do ripples out from you.

I've often told people who undertake personal transformation about the *times-ten principle*. It works on the basis that the change in your own vibration will flow to the people closest to you, maybe ten, maybe more. They will see the change and be inspired by you, perhaps enough to undertake their own journey. Relationships in your personal life, working life, and so on will all change for the better.

Remember the Maharishi Effect that we spoke of earlier, which describes how a group of people meditating can lower the crime rate in a major city? When you make decisions or take actions, they flow to all corners of your personal universe as well. Simply pause and send inspiration, healing, and courage to all your other selves. Ask one of your other selves to come forward and help you; you may be surprised by what happens. So often now, I follow one of the quantum echoes out into my personal universe when another self is calling. Simply set the intention for a wonderful interaction that benefits both you and your other self.

The way that we will change this planet is for more of us to send the ripples that evolve our quantum consciousness and take that evolution out into the fabric of the cosmos.

4. Hold Intention for a Better World

Engage your creator effect to manifest something amazing and remarkable for humanity. As you hold this pure and high vibration, it will change the energy that you send to others and the energy that moves through your personal universe. Ultimately, there are too many pessimists and not enough optimists. You know the people I refer to—it makes for a sad world when they hold the belief that there is danger everywhere and nothing is as good as it seems. For people like this, life becomes one long self-fulfilling prophecy.

There is another way.

See the beauty around you.

Look into the eyes of someone you love and see the miracle of life.

Walk through a forest and connect with the trees.

Hold a puppy, hug a child, raise your face to the sunlight and draw the energy into your being.

Tell stories that inspire whenever you can. Borrow and pass on life-changing books.

Tell people you love them, as though you were to never see them again. Make someone feel special, not just on their birthday.

Offer a random act of kindness to a stranger. You will be surprised how good that feels.

Most of all, do it as only you can, celebrating your uniqueness.

Remember one really important thing: your soul came here to be you in this time, this place, this body in the sacred symbiotic relationship of a spiritual being having a human experience. You were chosen by your soul from over seven billion options on this planet alone. I believe that this is the greatest act of unconditional love that any of us will ever experience.

Be grateful, give thanks ... and make a difference.

5. Say No in an Ever-Increasing Magnitude

Every change of significance starts at the smallest scale.

Hold at your very core, your subatomic particles, your being a vision for a different world, and it will come. We know the physical rules of cause and effect do not hold true at the quantum level. So bring your creator effect in, intangle with your other selves, be in your everywhereness, and do it all holographically.

Change is also about saying no. You actually have a choice and you can break patterns and conditioning by simply saying one word and carrying that through to your actions. You can move past the restrictive prevailing mindsets that ooze materialism, separation, and fear.

As you hold the higher intention and explore your unlimited potential, you will live a life in alignment with your vision.

Say no to the bombarding of your senses with advertising—simply mute the TV during ad breaks.

Say no to a political party that has the wrong policies—vote differently.

Say no to genetically modified foods—grow some of your own vegetables or herbs.

Say no to "medication only" mindsets—also pursue natural remedies.

Say no to relationships that drain your energy—change your approach to the person or simply move on.

Say no to the next purchase that you don't really need—just keep the old one a while longer.

There are a million different things you can do that start to change your world.

So in summary...

Explore your deeper self and your full potential courageously. Hold a better intention for our world and ripple that out holographically. Say no to the things in your life that draw on your conditioning or patterns that hold you back from being the amazing multi-dimensional being you already are.

Just remember who you are...

There is a chance you have been drawn to this book for a reason, and whatever that is, thank you for taking the time to read it.

Many souls are here at this time to make a difference, and you are likely to be one of these. It occurs to me that we are a planet short of gratitude at times, so may I, on behalf of all of humanity, simply say—thank you.

Remember who you are, because when you do, you draw on the higher collective purpose that is bringing the healing souls back to this planet at this time. As you shine, others will find you and come together in a wave of consciousness that can change this reality as we know it. All of this will happen easily as you remember who you are.

I offer you some words that may help at times. Read them over on tough days and remember the light is always there and cannot be extinguished—it is just that sometimes we don't remember.

The Lightworkers

We come to help a troubled world
As beings full of light
We choose to shine from loving realms,
Bring daylight to the night

We know that we will serve this world,
Because we have been shown
We recognize the others here
And know we aren't alone

Every now and then I know,
I need to go within
To build my light, empower my soul
And silence earthly din

And from my deep Remembering,
Comes a wave of inspiration
That ripples from my universe,
Bringing sacred transformation

In final gratitude, I mention this beautiful planet, known as Earth, Gaia, and many other names. She continues to nurture and sustain us in our journey through life. Without her, we would not have the opportunity to learn, grow, evolve, and remember who we really are.

RESOURCES

For more information on the Institute for Quantum Consciousness, our research updates, public events, facilitator trainings, and, most importantly, our accredited quantum consciousness facilitator network internationally, please go to www.institute-forquantumconsciousness.com.

Peter Smith's personal websites are www.quantumconscious ness.com.au and www.lblaustralia.com.au.

For more information on Life Between Lives hypnotherapy, please visit the Newton Institute at www.newtoninstitute.org. This organization, founded by Dr. Michael Newton, shares a listing of certified Life Between Lives hypnotherapists in forty countries around the world. This network of therapists and the trainings of the Newton Institute are the only ones supported and endorsed by Dr. Michael Newton.

BIBLIOGRAPHY

Alexander, Eben. *Proof of Heaven: A Neurosurgeon's Journey into the Afterlife*. Waterville, ME: Thorndike Press, 2013.

Beck, Don Edward, and Christopher Cowan. *Spiral Dynamics: Mastering Values, Leadership and Change*. Malden, MA: Blackwell Publishing, 1996.

Bible. New International Version. Colorado Springs, CO: Biblica, 2011. https://www.biblica.com/bible.

Blake, William. "Auguries of Innocence." In *The Complete Poetry & Prose of William Blake*. Edited by David V. Erdman. Revised ed. Berkeley: University of California Press, 1982.

Braden, Gregg. *The Divine Matrix: Bridging Time, Space, Miracles, and Belief*. Carlsbad, CA: Hay House, 2007.

Buddha. "The Twin Verses." In *The Dhammapada*. Edited by Friedrich Max Müller. Vol. 10 of *The Sacred Books of the East*. London: Claredon Press, 1881.

Conn Henry, Richard. "The Mental Universe." *Nature* 436 (July 2005), 29. doi:10.1038/436029a.

Covey, Stephen. *The 7 Habits of Highly Effective People*. New York: Simon and Schuster, 1989.

Greene, Brian. *The Fabric of the Cosmos: Space, Time, and the Texture of Reality*. New York: Penguin Books, 2004.

Hay, Louise. *Heal Your Body*. Carlsbad, CA: Hay House, 1988.

Hawkins, David. *Power vs. Force: The Hidden Determinants of Human Behavior*. Carlsbad, CA: Hay House, 1995.

Hicks, Esther, and Jerry Hicks. *Ask and It is Given: Learning to Manifest Your Desires*. Carlsbad, CA: Hay House, 2004.

Krishnamurti, J. "You Are the World." First public talk at Brandeis University, October 18, 1968. J. Krishnamurti Online. http://www.jkrishnamurti.org/krishnamurti-teachings/view-text.php?tid=19&chid=68560.

Lipton, Bruce. *The Biology of Belief: Unleashing the Power of Consciousness, Matter & Miracles*. Carlsbad, CA: Hay House, 2005.

Mafi, Maryam, trans. "178." In *Rumi Day by Day*. Charlottesville, VA: Hampton Roads Publishing, 2014.

McTaggart, Lynne. *The Field: The Quest for the Secret Force of the Universe*. London, UK: HarperCollins, 2001.

Moody, Raymond., Jr. *Life After Life: The Investigation of a Phenomenon—Survival of Bodily Death*. New York: HarperCollins, 2001.

Moore, David W. "Three in Four Americans Believe in Paranormal." Gallup News Service, June 16, 2005. https://home.sandiego.edu/~baber/logic/gallup.html.

Newton, Michael. *Destiny of Souls: New Case Studies of Life Between Lives*. St. Paul, MN: Llewellyn, 2001.

———. *Journey of Souls: Case Studies of Life Between Lives*. St. Paul, MN: Llewellyn, 1994.

———. *Life Between Lives: Hypnotherapy for Spiritual Regression*. St. Paul, MN: Llewellyn, 2004.

Rumi. "You, You, You." In *Love's Ripening: Rumi on the Heart's Journey*. Translated by Kabir Helminski and Ahmad Rezwani. Boston: Shambhala Publications, 2008.

Smith, Peter. *Hypnoenergetics—The Four Dimensions: An Overview of the New Approach to Hypnotherapy That Is Inspiring People Around the World*. Victoria, Australia: Barker Deane, 2011.

Talbot, Michael. *The Holographic Universe*. New York: HarperCollins 1996.

Von Däniken, Erich. *Chariots of the Gods?* London: Corgi Books, 1972.

Wolf, Fred Alan. *Parallel Universe: The Search for Other Worlds*. New York: Simon and Schuster, 1988.

To Write the Author

If you wish to contact the author or would like more information about this book, please write to the author in care of Llewellyn Worldwide, and we will forward your request. Both the author and publisher appreciate hearing from you and learning of your enjoyment of this book and how it has helped you. Llewellyn Worldwide cannot guarantee that every letter written to the author can be answered, but all will be forwarded. Please write to:

Peter Smith
℅ Llewellyn Worldwide
2143 Wooddale Drive
Woodbury, MN 55125.2989

Please enclose a self-addressed stamped envelope for reply,
or $1.00 to cover costs. If outside the USA,
enclose an international postal reply coupon.

GET MORE AT LLEWELLYN.COM

Visit us online to browse hundreds of our books and decks, plus sign up to receive our e-newsletters and exclusive online offers.

- Free tarot readings • Spell-a-Day • Moon phases
- Recipes, spells, and tips • Blogs • Encyclopedia
- Author interviews, articles, and upcoming events

GET SOCIAL WITH LLEWELLYN

Find us on  🐦 @LlewellynBooks

www.Facebook.com/LlewellynBooks

GET BOOKS AT LLEWELLYN

LLEWELLYN ORDERING INFORMATION

Order online: Visit our website at www.llewellyn.com to select your books and place an order on our secure server.

Order by phone:
- Call toll free within the US at 1-877-NEW-WRLD (1-877-639-9753)
- We accept VISA, MasterCard, American Express, and Discover.

Order by mail:
Send the full price of your order (MN residents add 6.875% sales tax) in US funds plus postage and handling to: Llewellyn Worldwide, 2143 Wooddale Drive, Woodbury, MN 55125-2989

POSTAGE AND HANDLING
STANDARD (US):(Please allow 12 business days)
$30.00 and under, add $6.00.
$30.01 and over, FREE SHIPPING.

CANADA:
We cannot ship to Canada. Please shop your local bookstore or Amazon Canada.

INTERNATIONAL:
Customers pay the actual shipping cost to the final destination, which includes tracking information.

Visit us online for more shipping options.
Prices subject to change.

FREE CATALOG!

To order, call
1-877-
NEW-WRLD
ext. 8236
or visit our
website